CONTAINER GARDENING

Jane Courtier

TIME
LIFE
BOOKS

Alexandria, Virginia

Time-Life Books is a division of Time Life Inc.

TIME LIFE INC.
CHAIRMAN AND CEO JIM NELSON
PRESIDENT AND COO STEVEN L. JANAS

TIME-LIFE TRADE PUBLISHING
VICE PRESIDENT AND PUBLISHER NEIL LEVIN
SENIOR DIRECTOR OF ACQUISITIONS AND
 EDITORIAL RESOURCES JENNIFER PEARCE
DIRECTOR OF NEW PRODUCT DEVELOPMENT CAROLYN CLARK
DIRECTOR OF TRADE SALES DANA HOBSON
DIRECTOR OF MARKETING INGER FORLAND
DIRECTOR OF CUSTOM PUBLISHING JOHN LALOR
DIRECTOR OF SPECIAL MARKETS ROBERT LOMBARDI
DIRECTOR OF DESIGN KATE L. McCONNELL
PROJECT MANAGER JENNIE HALFANT
COVER DESIGN JODY BILLERT

Originated in Singapore by Master Image
Printed and bound in China by Excel Printing

Books produced by Time-Life Trade Publishing are available
at a special bulk discount for promotional and premium use.
Custom adaptations can be created to meet your
specific marketing goals. Call 1-800-323-
5255.

10 9 8 7 6 5 4 3 2 1

ISBN 0-7370-1151-3

Library of Congress Cataloging-in-Publication Data
The Library of Congress has catalogued the trade version of this
title as follows:
Courtier, Jane.
  Container gardening / Jane Courtier.
    p. cm. -- (Time-Life garden factfile)
  ISBN 0-7370-0606-4 (spiral binding : alk. paper)
  1. Container gardening. I. Title. II. Series.

SB418 .C68 2000
635.9'86--dc21   99-040071

A Marshall Edition
Produced for Marshall Editions by PAGEOne, Cairn House,
Elgiva Lane, Chesham, Buckinghamshire, HP5 2JD

FOR PAGEOne
Art Director Bob Gordon
Editorial Director Helen Parker
Editor Charlotte Stock
Art Editor Suzanne Tuhrim
Picture Research Nadine Bazar
Photography Peter Anderson, Steve Wooster
Illustrations Karen Gavin

FOR MARSHALL EDITIONS
Managing Editor Anne Yelland
Managing Art Editor Helen Spencer
Editorial Director Ellen Dupont
Art Director Dave Goodman
Editorial Coordinator Ros Highstead
Production Nikki Ingram, Anna Pauletti

Measurements are given in imperial, followed by the metric
 equivalent in parentheses. Use one or the other when
  doing work, as the two measurements are not exactly
  equivalent.

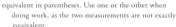

CONTENTS

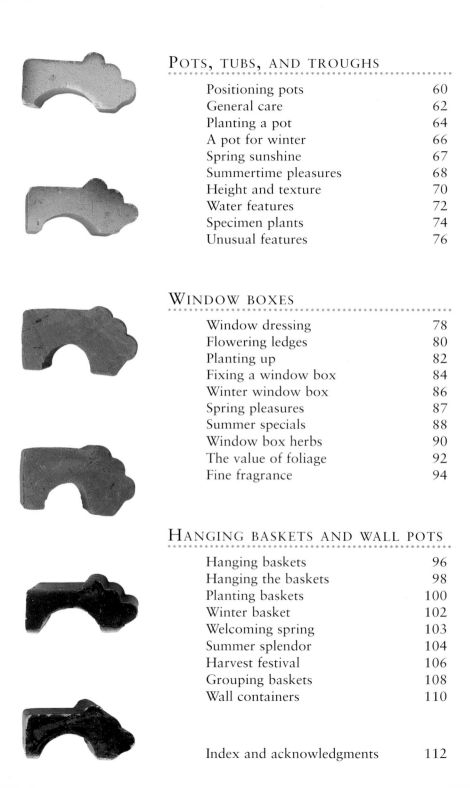

INTRODUCTION

Growing plants in containers is perhaps one of the most rapidly expanding areas of gardening. The general trend for small gardens has helped containers to achieve greater importance – they are always likely to have more impact in a confined area than in a large, spreading garden, and with only a small space to plant up and care for, we may feel we can afford to "splash out" on some really special containers for the plants. Containers also enable homeowners who have no garden at all to enjoy the pleasures of growing plants. Some of the most eye-catching and colorful displays are provided by window boxes, hanging baskets, and wall pots, bringing to life the exteriors of buildings.

CHOOSING CONTAINERS

The growing idea of treating the garden or patio as an extension of the house – effectively, an "outdoor room" – has encouraged more careful planning to achieve stylish effects, using attractive containers as the "furniture." Manufacturers have been swift to respond to the interest in container gardening, and a vast range of high-quality products is available in all shapes, sizes, and styles.

PLANTING AND GROWING

No matter how beautiful the
container, it needs plants to bring
it to life. Choosing the right plants,
and, just as importantly, knowing
how to care for them and achieve
the best from them, is vital if you
are to enjoy your container garden
to the fullest.

This book will give you the
guidance you need to make your containers
a success, with tried-and-tested ideas for
planting up and caring for plants in
a whole range of containers. But never be afraid
to experiment for yourself. One of the beauties of
container gardening is that it is easy and relatively
inexpensive to completely redesign your container
garden next season if you are not satisfied with the
results of this season's efforts!

Choosing containers

CHOOSING CONTAINERS

A wonderful and overwhelming selection of containers awaits anyone about to embark on container gardening. The range varies from plain and simple plastic pots, which even the smallest budget can afford, to stunningly beautiful and highly individual pieces of sculpture. In between are countless pots, tubs, troughs, and baskets in many different sizes, colors, shapes, and styles – surely something to suit everyone.

Plant containers are chosen not just for their looks – important though their appearance is. They must also be suitable for the plants that will grow in them, allowing room for roots to develop, good drainage, and the proper degree of insulation from severe weather. A careful balance between elegance and practicality is the keystone of the successful container garden.

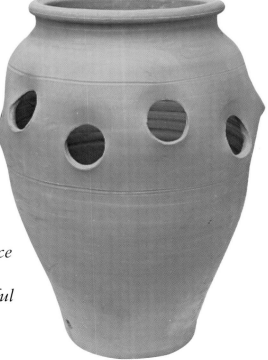

CONTAINER GROWING

In the natural world, most plants grow in soil in the open ground. But as long as a plant can get a ready supply of water and nutrients, it is not really fussy where it puts down its roots. Any object that can hold sufficient soil to allow the roots to expand and support the plant's topgrowth is a potential plant container.

WHY USE POTS?

There are many reasons why we need, and like, to grow plants in containers. In courtyard gardens where there may be no natural soil for plants to grow or in homes that have no garden at all, the beauty of plants can still be enjoyed in wall pots, window boxes, and hanging baskets, which can equally turn a balcony or roof area into a living garden. There are many advantages to container growing in any garden:

■ **Flexibility** Plants in containers can be moved around to give different effects or used in groupings.

■ **Focal point** The container itself can be an object of beauty or can be chosen to show off a special plant.

■ **Close inspection** Container plants can be displayed in a raised position, where their fine detail and their scent can be more readily appreciated.

■ **Young and old** Small children and older, less flexible gardeners enjoy the easy access of container gardens.

■ **Made to measure** The limited root space in a container restricts the overall size of many plants, allowing potentially large plants to be enjoyed in a small garden, whereas they would soon outgrow their space if raised in the open ground.

■ **Keeping trim** The more controlled growth often makes pruning and shaping plants easier, too.

■ **Prompt rewards** Containers are often quick and easy to plant: there is no backbreaking soil preparation required. Gardeners in a hurry can plant up containers to give instant results, using bedding plants that are about to bloom. An afternoon's easy work can produce a garden filled with color, which looks as though it has been established for weeks.

Containers can be planted up with trees, shrubs, and perennials that will thrive for many years, but most are used to display plants that last for just one season. This makes it easy to change the entire look of the garden every year or even every season.

SPECIAL SOILS

Pre-packaged commercial soil mix is easier to handle and is often of better quality than garden soil, giving more consistent results from plants. If you live in an area with lime-rich soil but long to raise lime-hating plants in your garden, grow them in containers of special ericaceous soil mix.

IN SUN AND SHADE
The versatility of containers means that they can be sited to suit the need of most plants, either sun lovers or shade dwellers.

CONTAINER MATERIALS

Pots, tubs, and baskets are available in a variety of materials. Which one you choose will depend mainly on the style of your existing garden and house, your own preferences, and your budget. As far as plants are concerned, the type of material the container is made from is usually less important than its size and shape.

TRADITIONAL POTS

Color and texture are the key differences between the materials most commonly used in containers.

TERRA-COTTA
CONTAINER

■ **Terra-cotta** The wide range in price of terra-cotta containers, in their familiar warm, brick-red shade, depends on their size and design. Clay is porous, which can provide good growing conditions for plants, but it also means that clay containers are likely to break up in freezing weather unless they are guaranteed frostproof. They are also fragile and will shatter if dropped. Glazed earthenware containers, which are often finished in bright colors or a pattern, are rarely guaranteed frostproof.

DECORATED
CERAMIC POT

■ **Wood** Tubs and troughs made from softwood are best treated with a plant-proof wood preserver to prevent rot. Good quality hardwood containers are made from kiln-dried timber to reduce shrinkage problems and have a longer life expectancy. If you choose a barrel, screw the metal hoops into place to prevent the tub from collapsing if it dries out.

■ **Stone** Natural stone comes in a range of colors and finishes and it weathers quickly to give an attractive "aged" effect. Stone containers are heavy and not suitable for moving around in the garden frequently or for balancing on ledges or balconies. They are surprisingly easy to damage unless treated carefully.

GLAZED
URN

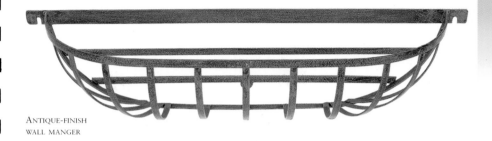

ANTIQUE-FINISH
WALL MANGER

LOOK-ALIKES

Where weight, budget, and weather-resistance are important factors in your choice of container, imitation materials offer an attractive solution.

■ **Concrete** Commonly used to imitate natural stone, concrete is not quite as realistic as reconstituted stone. It is used to make a range of relatively inexpensive, heavyweight containers. Straightforward, simple shapes are the most effective style of pot, and are preferable to many of the whimsical designs offered.

■ **Reconstituted stone** Made from crushed stone chips mixed with concrete, this material is not as attractive as real stone, but it is considerably less expensive. Like genuine stone, it is heavy and unwieldy, and containers are likely to break if dropped or mistreated.

■ **Metal** Containers made of metal may be galvanized or treated to mimic antique lead. They are best used as outer covers for lightweight pots, with the inside lined or treated to prevent rusting. Wall mangers are an attractive alternative to wall pots.

■ **Plastic** Containers made of plastic are inexpensive and easy to handle. A matt finish and stylish detail can give them a very convincing appearance, especially terra-cotta look-alikes. Being lightweight, plastic containers are prone to toppling over and break easily with age.

■ **Fiberglass** Used to mimic stone, metal, or wood, fiberglass is light-weight and tends to be tougher than plastic. Fiberglass containers are easily blown over in strong winds and should be weighted down.

Stylish matt finish

Broad base reduces risk of overbalancing

PLASTIC
CONTAINER

CONTAINER STYLES

Because plants will grow in almost anything that will hold soil, the possible styles and types of container are almost endless. Whether you are looking to decorate a large expanse of wall, a patio area, or a window sill, there is a pot to suit your site.

POTS AND BASKETS

Probably the most familiar type of container, pots range from the simple, standard-shaped flowerpot to large patio tubs, planters, and troughs. The standard pot shape is round, with the sides tapering slightly toward the base, making it easier to slide a plant out of its container when repotting.

Large wicker baskets make ideal patio tubs, while a hanging basket adds interest and height in any garden. The traditional basket is an open-dish shape made from

PUNCH BOWL
ON PLINTH

*Stem can be concealed
with trailing plants*

BASKET
PILLAR

a network of plastic-covered wire, and hung on chains. Plants are positioned in the top as well as through the sides of the basket to give an all-round effect that covers the basket (see p. 100). Variations include square, slatted-wood baskets, rigid metal baskets with lengthwise slits, and freestanding tiers of baskets held by a central pillar. Remember that all wire baskets need a liner to retain the soil. Solid-sided baskets are often fitted with a saucer, making them easier to plant up and less prone to drying out.

FOR WALLS AND LEDGES

There are several types of container designed to suit homes without any growing space, or where hardstanding is limited.

■ **Wall pots** A display of wall pots helps to give a three-dimensional effect to a garden and makes good use of all available space. Wall pots are generally small, and may be rectangular, half round, or almost completely round, with one side flattened to allow them to be fixed against a wall. Decorative versions add interest to plain walls and containers made in the form of heads, hands, or animal masks can provide an element of fun.

■ **Window boxes** Long, rectangular containers, usually of wood or plastic, are intended for display on window ledges. They can either be held by brackets, or the boxes may

WICKER HORN OF PLENTY

fit inside a decorative outer case, which is firmly fixed in position (see pp. 84–85). Shallow wooden and stone troughs are ideal for shallow-rooted alpine plants and can be used as window boxes or displayed in freestanding trough holders.

NOVELTY CONTAINERS

All manner of unusual items can be turned into containers, limited only by your ingenuity and, frequently, your sense of humor. It is usually old and worn-out objects that find a new lease on life as plant containers: wheelbarrows, chimney pots, sinks, tires, logs, – even old boots and lavatory pans have been planted up. Provided that there is adequate drainage and sufficient soil you should succeed. Experiment with objects of little or no value, so that they can, if necessary, be thrown away at the end of the season.

CERAMIC FROG PLANTER

MAKING A CHOICE

No matter how handsome the container, its appearance will be ruined by plants that are failing to thrive, or that are ill suited to its shape. To avoid disappointment, it is best to prepare a checklist of practical considerations so that you find the right pot for the right site. If you really can't resist an elegant but impractical piece, treat it as an ornament and leave it unplanted.

THINKING AHEAD

It is all too easy to select a container just because it is beautiful, without giving too much thought to its suitability for growing plants.

■ **Weight** The portability of a container is an important consideration, especially if you intend to change its position in the garden at regular intervals.

■ **Size** Any container must hold sufficient volume of soil or soil mix to support the plant for at least one season – longer if it is a perennial planting. It must also balance the topgrowth of the plant, so that it is not likely to become top heavy and fall over.

■ **Shape** It is not just the volume of soil that a container holds that is important; it is the ratio of its surface area to its depth. A wide, shallow sink may hold exactly the same amount of soil mix as a tall, slender pot, but the soil mix in the sink will dry out more rapidly and be of little value to a plant that has a deep, penetrating taproot. Shallow containers suit only shallow-rooted plants such as alpines and short-term bedding plants – even then they are likely to need frequent watering. Deep containers are essential for trees, shrubs, and perennials that have a long life expectancy.

DRAINAGE

It is vital that surplus water can drain away from the soil mix in containers; if the roots become waterlogged, the plant will die. In the open ground, water has plenty of opportunity to seep away, but in the restricted space of a container it can easily become trapped, and the effects of overwatering soon become evident.

Plastic containers often have several small drainage holes around the edge of the base; in stone and clay containers there may be one large, central hole. If the container has no drainage holes, it may be possible to add them yourself; otherwise place a deep layer of broken rubble at the base as a reservoir for excess water.

AWKWARD SHAPES

Choose fancy containers carefully as they may be impractical when it comes to planting or repotting. The necks of some tall pots, such as ali-baba jars, are narrower than the waists. This gives an elegant appearance, but makes it impossible to remove plants for repotting once their roots have grown into the widest area. Sometimes this problem can be overcome by setting a separate pot to contain the plant in the top of the jar, where it will be concealed, but can be lifted out easily.

PICK 'N' MIX POTS
A collection of containers in a variety of shapes
and styles and made from different materials
makes an attractive grouping on a patio.

Woven and wire containers drain
very freely and demand more
attention to watering than others.
Hanging baskets and wall pots hold
a large number of plants in a small
area, and so need frequent watering
and supplementary feeding during
the season to keep them at their best.

Warning

Check that your container is made
from plant-friendly material. Some
treated wooden or metal tubs may
contain chemicals that are toxic to
plants: if you are in any doubt, line
the containers with plastic sheeting
or seal them with bitumen-based
paint to prevent minerals or chemicals
from seeping into the soil mix.

POINTS TO CONSIDER

As well as being pleasing to look at and effective plant holders, containers need to suit your requirements, the size and situation of your garden, and the style or effect that you want to achieve. The most important consideration of all is that they should not demand any more of your time than you are able to spare.

TIME AND EFFORT

One advantage of a container garden is its flexibility; it allows you to reposition the containers and change their plants around to achieve a new look. You will often want to bring forward a plant when it is at its best, and return it to a less prominent position when its moment of glory is over. If you are growing short-term plants such as seasonal bedding, the

SHALLOW
DISH OF HERBS

containers will also need to be cleared out and replanted regularly. These tasks will be made much easier if you choose containers that are easy to lift, so opt for models that are moderately light in weight and not too large to handle.

If you intend to use plants that will stay in place for years, then stone troughs and heavy, awkward items present less of a problem. For gardeners with little time on their hands, a few large containers will require less attention than lots of small ones, and laborsaving ideas such as self-watering containers are worth considering.

STAYING PUT
Once a large pot has been planted up, it becomes quite an obstacle to move. Make sure that you are happy with its position before filling with soil mix and planting up.

PAIRING UP

The size and shape of the container should complement the plant growing in it (and vice versa). An elegant, statuesque container is usually most satisfying when balanced by a tall, graceful plant; while an intricate design on an ornate pot will be wasted if it is obscured by the foliage and flowers of trailing plants.

Some gardeners may be prepared to choose the container first and select the plants to suit it, but if you have a strong idea of the type of plants you want to grow, choose the containers with those plants in mind. To do justice to an arrangement of mixed plants, choose a wide-necked container or trough. If you want to grow tall plants that will need support, make sure that the container is deep enough to hold the base of the support firmly.

CLIMATE AND LOCATION

Variations in climate and prevailing weather conditions can have a considerable impact on certain types of containers; indeed, some are better suited to particular regions and areas. For example, heavy, stable items are more practical on a windswept site; wooden planters will need more frequent weatherproofing when used in exposed and coastal areas.

In areas that experience severe winters, choose frostproof containers with thick walls that will provide some protection for plant roots. Look for containers that offer good insulation for the roots when growing plants in a baking hot, sunny position, as it will help to keep the roots cool and moist. Small and shallow containers should be avoided in such a situation, as they dry out very rapidly.

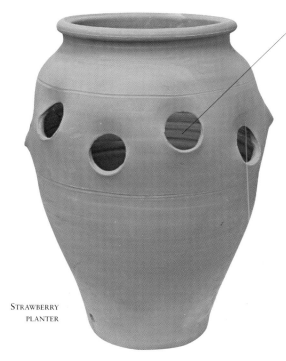

Fruits are trained through planting pockets

STRAWBERRY
PLANTER

STRAWBERRY PLANTERS

If you would like to try growing something for your kitchen, you might like to consider using a terra-cotta strawberry planter. These containers are fitted with side planting pockets through which herbs or strawberries can be trained. Provided that the plants are fed and watered regularly, you can count on a healthy crop each summer.

WHICH POT WHERE?

The beauty of containers is that they are equally at home in the country or the city, on the grounds of a large classical mansion or on the terrace of an ultramodern apartment building. To achieve the best possible effect in a chosen location, bear these points in mind.

POSITIONING CONTAINERS

Plants play an important role in linking a house with its garden; they help to soften hard landscaping and add color, fragrance, and interest. When grown in containers they can be kept tidy and under control more easily than in the open garden and fulfil the role of outdoor "furniture."

■ **Patio** With its practical hard surface and proximity to the house, the patio tends to become an outdoor room. Freestanding pots, tubs, and troughs of all shapes and sizes all suit patios, according to the space available, while wall pots and hanging baskets can be used to decorate an adjoining wall or fence.

■ **Paths and steps** A few well-placed containers clustered at various points or sited at regular intervals along a plain garden path can improve its appearance greatly and mark out its route from a distance.

Wide flights of steps also form an ideal display area – raising plants often helps to increase their impact.

Most freestanding containers can be used on paths and steps, but they and their contents should be small and neat enough not to interfere with people's progress past them. Wall pots and window boxes can be particularly effective fixed to the tops of balustrades and handrails, but again must not present a hazard.

■ **Walls** In small gardens and where there is no growing space at all, walls are particularly important to increase the area available for plants. Wall pots and mangers, hanging baskets, and window boxes are the containers to be used here. They must all be fixed securely to the wall and positioned in such a way as to make routine maintenance tasks such as watering and deadheading easy.

■ **Balconies and roof gardens**
A balcony or roof garden is an ideal surface for plants, but it is important to assess the load-bearing capability of the area. Site lightweight freestanding pots at the strongest points (usually around the edges). Adorn bordering walls or railings with troughs and window boxes.

AN OLD BATHTUB ADDS INTEREST TO A FORGOTTEN CORNER OF A GARDEN

ROOFTOP TERRAIN
Exposed to strong daytime sun, this rooftop garden provides the desert-like conditions enjoyed by cactuses and succulents.

GARDEN STYLES

There are no hard-and-fast rules about the correct use of containers in garden design – it is all a matter of personal preference. Whether your containers blend harmoniously with the garden style or provide a complete contrast, full of impact – both are equally effective.

SETTING THE TONE

Many gardens do not have a particular style of their own, and in small gardens especially, it is often the containers that will set the style. A distinct style can be achieved by selecting containers made from one type of material. A mixture of different materials tends to give an unsettled look but can be effective where an informal look is required. Generally, the most restful and pleasing effects are obtained by suiting containers to the style of your garden; bold contrasts require more courage and artistic flair to succeed. The material and style of the house is another factor to consider. An informal garden is more appropriate than a starkly modern design for a country cottage, and the regular lines of a formal garden suit a classical style house. Many gardens will fall into one of these categories.

■ **Formal** A formal style is made up of regular, symmetrical shapes and straight lines. The types of plants used may include clipped shrubs and topiary shapes, regular beds bordered by low hedging, and color-themed plantings. The overall impression is of neatness and regularity.

In a formal garden, containers should be made from one material, or just two or three different but blending materials. Matching pairs are essential when used to flank a doorway or to line a path.

■ **Informal** An informal style makes use of flowing lines and irregular forms rather than hard edges and symmetrical shapes. Plants are allowed to billow and mingle and are not kept rigidly clipped and shaped. Garden paths are more likely to meander than march straight through the center of the plot.

A TASTE OF MOROCCO
Hot, spicy colors, cool blue water, and ali baba-style containers conjure up the exotic, sultry charms of a Moroccan courtyard.

SPRING GREENS
The look of a traditional kitchen garden
is translated into the modern style by
the bold lines of this aluminum trough.

A mixture of styles and types of
container suits an informal setting,
with mixed groups of odd numbers
rather than rows of matching pots.

■ **Practical** Containers can be used
with great success for growing
a wide range of fruit and vegetables
(see pp. 36–37); even hanging
baskets and window boxes can
provide salad crops and herbs, and
the delights of early strawberries.
Straightforward plastic containers
or rustic-style earthenware usually
look more appropriate than classical,
highly ornamental containers.

■ **Classical** Stone balustrades,
Greco Roman-style urns and vases
on stone plinths and pedestals, all
in a strictly formal setting, help to
create a timeless classical style. Look
for containers with classical
decoration, such as lion masks,
acanthus, and foliage swags.
A fountain, bust, or sundial in
matching materials will further
enhance the classical theme.

■ **Modern** A modern style is
particularly suited to the town
gardens of contemporary buildings.
The clean, uncompromising lines of
bold, unornamented containers can
be very striking. Steel, fiberglass,
and plastic are common materials,
in either neutral or strong colors.

■ **Oriental** Glazed earthenware pots,
usually colorwashed and with a
Chinese- or Japanese-style design,
are very attractive and often
inexpensive. In a simple setting such
as a gravel garden, enhanced by
a sympathetic planting of bamboo
or Japanese maple, they can provide
a calm, relaxing atmosphere. A small
water feature (see pp. 72–73) will
add authenticity.

CREATING AN EFFECT

Once you have chosen your containers, you need to assess the best possible position for them in the garden to achieve maximum impact. In the right spot, containers can help to create illusions, altering the size and proportions of your garden area.

ANOTHER DIMENSION

A range of containers enables more than just one level to be used for growing plants. Window boxes, wall pots, and hanging baskets can be placed on adjacent surfaces for a three-dimensional effect. When a planting theme based on similar shades or textures is applied to all containers, it helps to link the surfaces together in a satisfying way. Extra interest will be added by using groups of containers to emphasize or create changes of level.

The hard angles of a patio and other paved areas can be softened by containers of flowing or trailing plants. The transition from a paved area to grass or flower borders can be smoothed by containers of plants placed where the two meet.

LARGE GARDENS

In a large garden, a container can prove useful as a focal point; for example, a grand, dramatically styled urn placed on a pedestal for extra height, and planted with a mixture of upright and trailing plants, will simply demand attention.

Containers may also be used as "pointers" to draw the eye to a feature, perhaps a flight of steps, or to a different aspect of the garden. They can also be used to make a garden's dimensions look different. Long, narrow plots appear wider if grouped containers are placed at intervals along both sides of the garden. By using pots that gradually decrease in size the farther away they are from the viewpoint, a small area can be made to look larger.

VISUAL TRICKS

• Unless the size of the container is deliberately being used to create optical illusions, it should be kept in scale with the area in which the container is sited. Very small containers will be lost in a large garden, and a grand, imposing container on a tiny patio can look ridiculously out of proportion.

• Avoid pairing a brilliant display of plants with a very striking, decorative container – they will vie with each other for attention and reduce impact.

• Sympathetic planting is essential. If the container is the main point of interest, the planting should be discreet but complementary. If the focus centers on a bold display of plants, a simple, neutral-colored container is usually the most effective. Delicate-looking foliage, such as ferns, is best offset against a plain terra-cotta pot.

LIVING SCREENS

Many gardens or balconies contain or overlook an object or area that is not particularly attractive. A group of container plants can be the perfect way to disguise an eyesore, forming a living screen that can be replaced, if necessary, as it dies down or passes its best. Containers can liven up a dull area of the garden temporarily – plants in full flower can be sunk in to the soil in their containers to boost up a border when it is needed. Later, when the border starts to come into its own, the container plants can be removed and used elsewhere.

TO THE POINT
Geometric, electric blue containers, raised on metal tripods, accentuate the striking spiky foliage of blue grass (Festuca glauca).

GROUPING CONTAINERS

Dotting odd containers here and there around the garden is never the best way to use them – they will have far more impact if several are grouped together. Grouping also makes regular tasks, such as watering, easier and will improve growing conditions for the plants.

Grouped pots do not have to be made from the same material, but the best effect is obtained if they are all of a similar shade and texture; red sandstone, brick, and terra-cotta blend harmoniously. Containers grouped in odd numbers – three, five, or seven – have a more satisfying appearance than groups of even numbers (unless they are lined up in pairs in a formal setting).

A triangular layout makes an effective arrangement. The apex of the triangle may be in the center of the group or to one side; if no pot is tall enough to form an apex, stand one of them on a concealed brick to give extra height. A wall pot or hanging basket could also be used to form the apex. Keep fluidity in the display by linking the plantings – either through a common color or by making their outlines "flow" from one container to the next.

PAINT EFFECT

• If your budget will not stretch to buying large numbers of the same container, or if you already have a wide selection of containers made from different materials, you can help to unify them to form groups by painting them.

• Unglazed terra-cotta and earthenware pots are easy to color with matt-finish paints; metal and plastic containers usually need coating with primer before applying the paint.

• Sand down glossy plastic to provide a key for the paint. Some of the best effects can be obtained by using two-toned colors to give a "distressed" effect; vary the emphasis of the colors within the group to avoid too regular an appearance.

HAND-PAINTED TIMBER TUB

Plants for containers

PLANTS FOR CONTAINERS

Some container plants give their all to provide a glorious show of color for a single season; others will survive to give pleasure for many years. The choice of suitable plants is extensive: architectural plants provide strong shapes and outlines; flowers and foliage supply a wide variety of color and form; softly flowing trailing plants make an effective contrast to stiffly upright specimens.

*   A pleasing balance of shape and form, texture, and color can be obtained from a mix of annuals, perennials, bulbs, shrubs, and trees. While the range of plants that will grow successfully in containers is surprisingly wide, it pays to know which ones adapt most happily to container growing.*

PLANT ESSENTIALS

Virtually any plant can be grown in a container for at least part of its life – but that does not mean that all plants are suitable or worthwhile for growing in a container garden. A look at the basic requirements of plants helps in our understanding of the part that containers play.

WHAT PLANTS NEED

2

All garden plants require water and dissolved minerals; air, containing oxygen and carbon dioxide; and light, which is converted into energy for development and growth.

In most instances, the water and mineral solutions that a plant needs for growth are supplied by soil, from where they are taken up by the plant's roots. The surface area of the roots is increased by the presence of millions of tiny root hairs that absorb moisture in the soil. As the root system spreads it provides a firm base for the plant, allowing the aerial parts to develop above the ground.

TAKING ROOT

Different types of plants have different types of root systems, varying from a single, large, deep-growing taproot to a shallow mat of many slender, branching roots.

Only a tiny amount of soil may be needed to keep a plant growing: weeds spring up through tarmac and paving, and alpine plants survive on pinches of soil in mountain crevices. However, once the supply of water and nutrients in the soil is exhausted, the plant dies. In general, the larger and more vigorous the plant, the more water and nutrients it needs to grow – and, in theory, the larger the volume of soil that is needed to supply them.

Leaves absorb oxygen and sunlight for growth and development.

Dissolved nutrients are carried up to the foliage by the plant's stem or trunk.

Plants take up water through their roots. The larger the plant, the bigger its root system, so the bigger the volume of soil it will require.

HALF-STANDARD *CUPRESSUS ARIZONICUS*

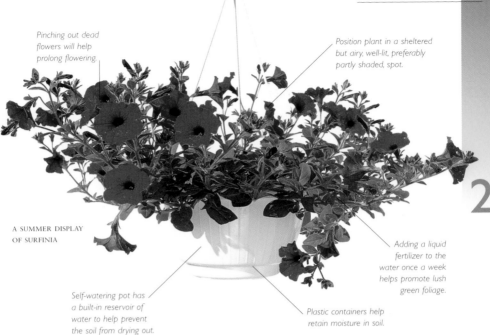

Pinching out dead flowers will help prolong flowering.

Position plant in a sheltered but airy, well-lit, preferably partly shaded, spot.

A SUMMER DISPLAY OF SURFINIA

2

Adding a liquid fertilizer to the water once a week helps promote lush green foliage.

Self-watering pot has a built-in reservoir of water to help prevent the soil from drying out.

Plastic containers help retain moisture in soil.

GROWING IN CONTAINERS

A plant container of any sort limits the volume of soil available to the roots. However, in a garden, we can make sure that a supply of water and nutrients always remains available to the plants, even after the soil's own supply has run out. Regular watering and the application of fertilizers can keep plants developing healthily for many months and even years.

Once a plant's roots become physically constricted by the lack of space in the container, the development of the topgrowth will be affected, too; while still healthy, growth will be slowed despite feeding and watering, and the plant will usually remain smaller than if grown in the open ground. This can often be a benefit, because it allows potentially large plants to be grown successfully in small gardens.

In other cases, however, a plant in a container may never be able to develop sufficiently to reach the stage at which it would become attractive, making it unsuitable for container growing. Very large, fast-growing trees and shrubs, and plants with deep taproots, are not usually the best choices for growing in containers, because the root will never manage to reach the depth it requires and growth will be stunted.

Some plants can be grown very happily for a single season in a container and are then fit only for throwing away; they are replaced by new plants in the following year. Others can be grown for several years in the same container, with just occasional repotting to keep them healthy and looking good (see p. 55).

Plants are often broadly grouped by their natural cycle of growth. The main categories are annuals and biennials; perennials; bulbs; and trees and shrubs. The next few pages highlight suitable container-friendly examples from each category.

ANNUALS AND BIENNIALS

When you are looking for an instant display of color and foliage to brighten up your garden throughout the summer season, look no further than the wide variety offered by annuals and biennials – the number-one choice for container gardens.

A SEASON OF FLOWERS

2

Most annuals and bedding plants are grown for their colorful flowers, although some are valued for their foliage. Their form may be bushy, spreading, or upright; trailing varieties spill over the sides of pots, baskets, and troughs, while climbers make good, fast-growing screens.

Many annuals, biennials, and bedding plants used to be sold only in mixed colors, but single shades are becoming more common, making effective color scheming possible.

An annual plant is one that grows from seed, flowers, and dies within a single-growing season; a biennial grows from seed in one season, overwinters, then flowers and dies the following season. Annuals and biennials can be further subdivided.

POPULAR ANNUALS AND BIENNIALS

HARDY ANNUALS	HALF-HARDY ANNUALS	BIENNIALS
Calendula officinalis Pot marigold	**Ageratum houstonianum** Floss flower	**Campanula medium** Canterbury bell
Centaurea cyanus Cornflower	**Antirrhinum majus** Snapdragon	**Dianthus barbatus** Sweet William
Clarkia amoena Satin flower	**Begonia semperflorens** Bedding begonia	**Matthiola incana** Brompton stock
Helichrysum bracteatum Everlasting flower	**Callistephus chinensis** China aster	**Althaea rosea** Hollyhock
Lathyrus odoratus Sweet pea	**Impatiens walleriana** Impatiens	**Bellis perennis** Double daisy
Nigella damascena Love-in-a-mist	**Papaver nudicaule** Iceland poppy	**Digitalis purpurea** Foxglove
Papaver rhoeas Shirley poppy	**Pelargonium** Bedding geranium	**Erysimum cheiri** Wallflower
Tropaeolum majus Nasturtium	**Phlox drummondii** Annual phlox	**Myosotis sylvatica** Forget-me-not
Viola × wittrockiana Pansy	**Portulaca grandiflora** Sun plant	**Viola × wittrockiana** **Floral Dance series** Winter-flowering pansy
	Salvia splendens Salvia	

*Evenly balanced
display of flowers*

*Trailing habit covers
underside of basket*

2

A CASCADE OF FUCHSIAS

■ **Hardy annuals** Fully hardy means
that plants can withstand frost, so
they can be sown at any time in the
spring, or sometimes in the preceding
fall for early flowering plants.

■ **Half-hardy annuals** Half-hardy
indicates that plants will be killed
by frost, so they must not be taken
outdoors until all risk of frost is over
in spring; their flowering season is
cut short by the first frosts in fall.

■ **Perennials treated as annuals** (or
biennials) Plants that fall under this
category botanically are not true
annuals or biennials – they do not
die after flowering – but they are
discarded at the end of their first
flowering season in the garden
because their appearance deteriorates
in their second and subsequent years.
Here, they may be referred to as
annuals or biennials for simplicity.

■ **Bedding plants** Bedding is a
general term used for many types of
annual and tender perennial that are
usually bought as young plants and
transplanted into the garden or
containers for one season only.

Bedding plants are discarded after
flowering, although some tender
perennials are worth overwintering
in a greenhouse or conservatory
to provide cuttings for the
following spring.

POPULAR CLIMBERS AND TRAILERS

CLIMBERS	TRAILERS
Convolvulus tricolor Convolvulus	**Anagallis monelli** Blue pimpernel
Eccremocarpus scaber Chilean glory flower	**Convolvulus sabatius**
Ipomoea tricolor Morning glory	**Fuchsia** Some varieties
Lathyrus odoratus Sweet pea	**Lobelia erinus** Lobelia
Thunbergia alata Black-eyed Susan	**Lotus berthelotii**
Tropaeolum majus Nasturtium	**Pelargonium peltatum** Ivy-leaf geranium
	Sutera grandiflora Purple glory plant
	Verbena x hybrida

PERENNIALS

The most familiar use for perennials is in perennial borders, but many species make excellent container plants. They are nowhere near as popular for container growing as bedding plants, and this is a shame, as they have great potential.

COLOR AND FOLIAGE

2

A perennial is a plant that persists from year to year; normally its topgrowth dies down in winter and new shoots appear from the crown at or below ground level in spring. A few perennials, such as euphorbia and bergenia, are evergreen, but tender perennials, which cannot withstand temperatures that fall to

below freezing, are often treated as annuals and simply discarded after their first flowering season; others can be kept from year to year as long as they are brought under cover in the winter. Commercial plant breeders have introduced a wide range of short, compact varieties of perennials, many of which are ideal for growing in containers.

Perennial plants tend to increase their spread over several seasons, which can present a problem where more than one plant occupies a container – a strong-growing plant will eventually swamp a weaker one. Growing perennials as single specimens in containers overcomes this problem; dramatic species such as spiky *Phormium tenax* or the golden foliage of hakonechloa make splendid candidates.

The flowering season for perennials runs from early or mid-summer to early fall; the foliage may persist for longer. The one drawback of growing perennials in containers is that they remain dormant over winter. This means that the containers cannot be planted up with winter and spring bedding. The best solution is to use a selection of perennials, combined with evergreen shrubs, to provide an extended season of interest.

SPIKES OF COLOR
Lupins grown in individual containers provide spikes of instant summer color, ranging from creamy yellow to delicious raspberry pink.

PERENNIALS FOR GROWING IN CONTAINERS

FLOWERING

Cosmos atrosanguineus
Chocolate cosmos

Dianthus species
Pinks

Diascia cordata and hybrids

Erysimum 'Bowles Mauve'

Geranium 'Johnson's Blue'
Cranesbill

Lysimachia 'Outback Sunset'
Loosestrife

Paeonia lactiflora
Peony

Penstemon hybrids

Phygelius aequalis
Cape figwort

Primula vulgaris
Primrose

DIANTHUS SPECIES

FOLIAGE

Ajuga reptans 'Multicolor'
Bugle

Alchemilla mollis
Lady's mantle

Arum italicum
Lords and ladies

Bergenia hybrids
Elephants' ears

Euphorbia amygaloides 'Purpurea'
Purple wood spurge

Festuca glauca
Blue grass

Hakonechloa macra 'Aureola'

Helichrysum petiolare

Helleborus argutifolius

Heuchera micrantha var. diversifolia 'Palace Purple'
Coral flower

Hosta species and cultivars
Plantain lily

Ophiopogon planiscapus 'Nigrescens'
Black grass

Stachys byzantina
Lambs' ears

Phormium tenax
New Zealand flax

TENDER
(Protect from frost)

Argyranthemum frutescens
Marguerite

Brugmansia sanguinea
Angels' trumpets

Canna hybrids
India shot plant

Dahlia cultivars

Gazania cultivars

Osteospermum cultivars

Tibouchina urvilleana
Brazilian spider flower

FALL FLOWERS

Aster novi-belgii
Michaelmas daisy

Chrysanthemum cultivars

Dahlia cultivars

Helenium autumnale
Sneezewort

Liriope muscari
Lilyturf

Sedum spectabile
Ice plant

WINTER INTEREST

Bergenia cordifolia
Elephants' ears

Euphorbia characias
Wood spurge

Festuca glauca
Blue grass

Lamium maculatum 'Beacon Silver'
Deadnetttle

Phormium tenax
New Zealand flax

Heuchera 'Pewter Moon'
Coral flower

2

FLOWERING BULBS

Bulbs are easy to plant, flower reliably in their first season, and make compact growth, so in many ways they are ideal for growing in containers. They can be mass planted to make a truly spectacular display for relatively little effort.

WHAT IS A BULB?

2

A bulbous plant is one in which part of the plant is swollen with a supply of stored food. This store enables the plant to survive dormancy and resume growth when conditions are right. Bulbous plants include bulbs, corms, tubers, and rhizomes, though it is sometimes difficult to tell them apart simply from their appearance.

■ **Bulb** A bulb consists of fleshy scales (modified leaves) attached to a basal plate and is often covered by dry, papery skin, or tunic. Narcissus, tulip, and hyacinth are all bulbs.

■ **Corms** From the outisde, corms look similar to bulbs but they are swollen stem bases, not scales.

Unlike a bulb, a corm disappears as its food supply is used up, and is replaced each year. Popular corms include crocus and freesia.

■ **Tubers** Like corms, tubers are also swollen stems, but unlike corms they do not have a basal plate – roots may grow all over the surface, and growth buds are carried at several points on the surface, too. Examples include cyclamen and begonia.

■ **Rhizomes** Rhizomes often grow horizontally at or just under the soil surface; border iris is probably the best-known type.

AFTERCARE

The main season of interest for bulbs is spring, although the earliest of these appear in winter, and there is a good selection of useful summer-flowering bulbs, too. Once bulbs have finished flowering they can be planted in open ground if space is available; leave the foliage until it dies down naturally to provide a food supply for next year's growth. Alternatively, bulbs can be discarded in the same way as bedding plants.

A mixed container planted with shrubs, bedding, or annuals, to take over once the bulbs have flowered can be successful, but remember to feed the bulbs with liquid fertilizer to ensure a repeat performance the following year.

SPRING-FLOWERING BULB

Nose of bulb

Protective paperlike skin

Basal plate

BULBS FOR ALL SEASONS

BULBS FOR WINTER

Chionodoxa luciliae
Glory of the snow

Crocus ancyrensis
Golden bunch crocus

Crocus tommasinianus

Cyclamen coum

Cyclamen persicum

Eranthis hyemalis
Winter aconite

Galanthus nivalis
Common snowdrop

Galanthus nivalis 'Flore Pleno'
Double common snowdrop

Iris danfordiae

Narcissus cyclamineus
Miniature daffodils

BULBS FOR SPRING

Anemone blanda

Convallaria majalis
Lily of the valley

Crocus chrysanthus

Erythronium dens-canis
Dog's tooth violet

Fritillaria imperialis
Crown imperial

Ornithogalum umbellatum
Star of Bethlehem

Hyacinthus orientalis
Hyacinth

Muscari azureum
Grape hyacinth

Narcissus cultivars
Daffodil

Tulipa cultivars
Tulip

BULBS FOR SUMMER

Allium species
Ornamental onion

Alstroemeria cultivars
Peruvian lily

Begonia x tuberhybrida

Canna hybrida
Indian shot

Dahlia cultivars

Gladiolus callianthus

Iris cultivars

Lilium species and cultivars

Ranunculus asiaticus
Persian buttercup

Rhodohypoxis baurii 'Douglas'

Tigridia pavonia
Peacock flower

BULBS FOR THE FALL

Amaryllis belladonna
Belladonna lily

Colchicum autummnale
Autumn crocus

Crocus speciosus

Crocus laevigatus

Cyclamen hederifolium

Dahlia cultivars

Leucojum autumnale
Autumn snowflake

Merendera montana

Nerine bowdenii

Schizostylis coccinea
Kaffir lily

Sternbergia lutea
Autumn daffodil

Zephyranthes candida
Rainflower

2

TULIPS IN A MIXED PLANTING

TREES AND SHRUBS

Whether grown as specimens or as a backdrop to colorful borders, trees and shrubs help to form the framework of a garden. This applies just as strongly to container gardens, where they can act as "reference points" around which to plan the rest of the planting.

SIZE MATTERS

The distinction between a tree and a shrub is not as clear-cut as it might first appear, as a degree of overlap exists between the categories. In general, trees have a single clear stem forming a trunk, while shrubs usually have several small stems arising from the base; trees are normally also taller than shrubs.

The majority of trees and shrubs will grow very large, which restricts their suitability for containers. Although their likely height and spread, and the extent of their root growth may rule them out as container plants, several species will make attractive short-term exhibits until they outgrow their container.

Shrubs and trees can be treated as single specimens or may share a tub with bulbs or bedding plants around their base to add extra color and extend their season. Some shrubs, such as hebe and erica, have small, neat forms that enable them to grow happily in medium-sized containers, for at least one season. Most trees and shrubs, though, are likely to stay put for several years, so choose a sturdy, weatherproof container.

STRUCTURE AND FOLIAGE

Permanent container plantings need to work hard to justify their place, so make sure they offer more than one feature of interest. Evergreens, which carry their leaves all year round, form a valuable background of foliage, especially in winter when there may be little else of interest in the garden. Deciduous trees and shrubs change with the seasons, bearing fresh new leaves in spring, offering cool shade in summer, and shedding their often fiery colored leaves in the fall, to reveal a striking network of branches during winter.

COOK'S DELIGHT
A small bay tree grown in a terra-cotta urn makes a handsome specimen, adding height and interest to a grouping of small foliage plants.

TREES AND SHRUBS AS SPECIMEN PLANTS

2

SMALL TREES

Acacia dealbata
Mimosa

***Acer palmatum* 'Dissectum'**
Japanese maple

Eucalyptus gunnii
Gum tree

***Juniperus scopulorum* 'Skyrocket'**

Laurus nobilis
Sweet bay

Magnolia stellata

***Malus* x *zumi* 'Golden Hornet'**
Crab apple

***Prunus* 'Kiku-shidare-zakura'**
Flowering cherry

***Pyrus salicifolia* 'Pendula'**
Weeping pear

***Salix caprea* 'Kilmarnock'**
Kilmarnock willow

Trachycarpus fortunei
Fan palm

SHRUBS

Camellia japonica
Camellia

Choisya ternata
Mexican orange blossom

Cotoneaster microphyllus

***Euonymus fortunei*
'Emerald 'n' Gold'**

Hydrangea macrophylla
Common hydrangea

Pieris japonica

Pyracantha watereri
Firethorn

***Skimmia japonica* 'Rubella'**

Viburnum tinus
Laurustinus

Vinca major
Periwinkle

***Weigela* 'Victoria'**

***Yucca gloriosa* 'Variegata'**

LOW-GROWING
COTONEASTER MICROPHYLLUS

CONTAINER FOODS

I t is surprising how many edible crops can be grown successfully in containers, which can be placed within easy reach of the kitchen. They won't yield a constant supply of summer produce, but they will contribute several interesting varieties to enjoy with your meal.

POTTED CROPS

2

To be a suitable candidate for container growing, the variety needs to be reasonably compact, without very deep or spreading roots, and it must be able to produce a worthwhile crop from a small number of plants. In order to earn its place in a small garden, the variety should also be attractive to look at; those offering bright flowers, striking foliage, or fall color as well as edible produce double their value.

FRUIT TIPS

Apple
• Varieties on dwarfing rootstocks such as M27 grow well in deep tubs.
• For single specimens, choose a family tree grafted with three different varieties.
• Ballerina and Minarette trees are columnar varieties specially raised for container growing.

Blueberry
• Orange and copper leaf color in the fall.
• Grow in large pots of lime-free soil mix.
• Choose 'Herbert' for the best flavor.

Cherry
• Dwarfing rootstock Inmil allows cherries to be grown in deep tubs.
• Self-fertile varieties include 'Stella', 'Sunburst', and 'Cherokee'.

Peach
• Dwarf varieties 'Bonanza', 'Garden Annie', 'Garden Lady', and 'Nectarella' (nectarine) are ideal for growing in deep tubs.
• Needs shelter from mid-winter to spring in cold climates.

Plum
• Suitable for growing in a deep tub.
• Grow trees on the dwarfing rootstock 'Pixy', which requires rich soil.
• Self-fertile varieties include 'Czar' (cooking plum), 'Denniston's Superb' (greengage), 'Opal', and 'Victoria.'

Strawberry
• Many different varieties, including small-fruited but tasty alpine types. Strawberries may crop

STRAWBERRY PLANTER

between early summer and fall, depending on variety.
• Suitable for growing bags, pots, window boxes, terra-cotta planters, and hanging baskets.
• The small fruits of alpine strawberries, such as 'Baron Solemacher,' are less prone to attack by birds.

VEGETABLE TIPS

Beans
• 'Purple Teepee' and 'Golddukat' have attractive colored pods.
• Suits window boxes, growing bags, and pots.
• Runner bean 'Hestia' is a dwarf variety for tubs, with red and white flowers.

Beetroot
• Suitable for growing in bags or tubs.
• Roots are best pulled at golf-ball size.
• 'Pronto' and 'Monaco' are good for pots and growing bags. 'Action' is ideal for baby beet.

Carrot
• Choose short-rooted varieties such as 'Amini' and 'Mignon', or globe-rooted 'Parmex', valued for its sweet taste.
• Suitable for raising in pots, growing bags, and window boxes.
• Take care not to overwater.

Eggplant
• Good for a warm, sheltered position.
• Bears up to six glossy, purple-black fruits during late summer.
• Try 'Bonica' or 'Mini Bambino' in a tub or growing bag.

Lettuce
• Try baby iceberg 'Blush', cut-and-come-again, frilly-leaved 'Frisby', or purple, crimped 'Lollo Rossa'.
• Suitable for raising in pots, growing bags, or window boxes.

Sweet pepper
• Pick fruits when green, or leave them until they are red, when they are fully ripe and sweet.
• 'Redskin' and 'Apache' are good container varieties for raising in pots or growing bags.

Tomato
• Small-fruited types, with cherry-sized fruits, are the most decorative.
• Try 'Totem' or 'Tornado' in pots or growing bags.
• Trailing variety 'Tumbler' suits hanging baskets.

Zucchini
• Produces large, rich yellow flowers.
• Different shapes and colors of fruit available.
• Bush varieties such as deep green 'Supremo' or golden 'Sunburst' suit growing bags or tubs.

2

CONTAINER-GROWN
KALE AND CHIVES

POPULAR PLANTS

Of the many container-friendly plants, some species and varieties are especially popular, valued for their particularly brilliant color, a graceful or compact habit of growth, ease of cultivation, resistance to pests and diseases, or a long and prolific flowering season. The following selection of popular plants includes new varieties as well as established favorites but all are reliable choices for containers.

2

POPULAR CONTAINER PLANTS

Ageratum houstonianum
Floss flower

A summer-flowering bedding plant with fluffy heads of purple-blue flowers forming a dome over the mid to dark green, oval, toothed leaves. Varieties include 'Blue Champion', 'Blue Horizon', 'Neptune', and 'Blue Mink'. Sow under cover in spring; plant out after frosts. Suitable for window boxes and tubs.
HEIGHT: 9 in (23 cm)

Antirrhinum majus
Snapdragon

Half-hardy annual bearing elegant, tapering spikes of lipped flowers in a range of colors and bicolors. Varieties include Crown and Coronette series; double-flowered 'Madame Butterfly'; and low-growing Magic Carpet and Candelabra groups – ideal for hanging baskets as well as tubs. Sow under cover in spring; plant out after frosts.
HEIGHT: 6–16 in (15–40 cm)

Begonia cultivars
Begonia

Two types of this half-hardy annual/tuber are popular for containers. The fibrous-rooted Semperflorens begonias have small, yellow-eyed flowers in red, pink, and white shades; the rounded foliage is often bronzy green. Devil, Super Olympia, and Victory series are reliable. Tuberhybrida begonias have large, showy blooms. The long-flowering Nonstop series is the most popular. Good for all containers; trailing types are especially useful in hanging baskets. Buy plants or tubers and plant them out after frosts. Keep soil just moist and provide good ventilation during winter.
HEIGHT: 6–12 in (15–30 cm)

Fuchsia cultivars
Fuchsia

A tender perennial/shrub bearing delicate, usually drooping flowers of distinctive shape, with colored petals and often contrasting colorful sepals. Hardy varieties make good tub plants; try the upright dwarf varieties of 'Tom Thumb' (very free-flowering) or 'Mrs Popple'. Fuchsias are commonly grown as frost-tender bedding plants. The trailing varieties are well suited to window boxes, hanging baskets, and troughs. Plant outside after frosts.
HEIGHT: 24–48 in (60–120 cm)

POTTED FUCHSIA

POPULAR CONTAINER PLANTS

Hedera helix
Ivy
A hardy climbing shrub with lobed leaves on sturdy climbing or trailing stems; there are many attractively variegated types such as 'Glacier', 'Harlequin', 'Gold Child', and 'White Knight'. Ivies are well suited to all types of container, especially when they are allowed to trail over the edge, or trained up stakes to give height. Green-edged varieties tolerate shade, but variegated ones prefer sun. Excellent winter interest, but attractive all year round. Set out young plants at anytime. Contact with the sap may irritate skin or provoke an allergy.
HEIGHT/SPREAD: indeterminate

TRAILING IVY

Helichrysum petiolare
Helichrysum
The long, trailing or arching stems of this tender shrub are clothed with felted, oval leaves of dusty silver. Its daisylike flowers are usually white or yellow. Popular varieties for hanging baskets include 'Limelight' (lemon-yellow foliage) and 'Roundabout' (small-leaved with cream variegation). Set out young plants after frost. Overwinter under cover to provide cuttings for the following spring.
HEIGHT/SPREAD: to 3 ft (to 90 cm)

Impatiens walleriana
Impatiens
This half-hardy annual has bronze-green foliage and produces flat-faced, spurred flowers in a wide range of colors. Impatiens are very free flowering and provide summer-long interest. They are tolerant of shade and suit all types of container. Reliable series include Accent, Tempo (some bicolors and picotees), and Super Elfin; Confection and Carousel series feature semidouble and double flowers. Sow in spring; plant out after frosts. Protect from cold winds.
HEIGHT: 6–10 in (15–25 cm)

Lobelia
Lobelia
Lobelia erinus is a half-hardy annual with small, lance-shaped or oval leaves and lipped flowers, usually in shades of blue. Plants are upright and bushy or trailing, according to variety. Riviera series (early flowering) and 'Crystal Palace' (dark green leaves) are bushy varieties; Regatta and Fountain (profuse flowers) series are good trailing plants. Easy to raise from seed in spring or buy as a bedding plant.
HEIGHT: 4–6 in (10–15 cm)
Lobelia tupa is a robust perennial with red-purple stems and fiery orange-red flowers. It makes a striking display in barrel gardens and large tubs.
HEIGHT: to 3 ft (to 1 m).

LOBELIA TUPA

2

2

POPULAR CONTAINER PLANTS

Nemesia strumosa
Nemesia

'Sundrops Mixed' and other modern selections of this half-hardy annual offer a wide range of bright shades and a prolonged flowering season. Nemesia is compact and rounded, free-flowering and early to come into bloom after planting out. It is suitable for growing in all types of containers. Transplant carefully to avoid root disturbance and keep well watered in dry spells.
HEIGHT: 6–8 in (15–20 cm)

Nicotiana hybrids
Tobacco plant

A half-hardy annual with trumpet-shaped flowers in shades of red, pink, salmon, and white. Old varieties have a strong fragrance but close their flowers in the middle of the day; modern varieties stay open all day but many have lost their scent. The Domino series has compact plants with flowers in a good color range; 'Lime Green' has unusual green flowers. For fragrance, try the taller 'Heaven Scent'. Plant out in spring in full sun or partial shade. Contact with the foliage may cause skin irritation.
HEIGHT: 10–24 in (25–60 cm)

Osteospermum cultivars
South African daisy

A tender perennial bearing large, daisylike flowers in an extensive range of colors. Varieties in the Starlight series are compact and early flowering; 'Pink Whirls' and 'Whirligig' have spoonshaped petals, which are rolled in the center; 'Silver Sparkler' has variegated foliage and white flowers. Good for raising in tubs. Choose a sunny position because the flowers tend to close in shade. Deadhead regularly to prolong the flowering period.
HEIGHT: 14 in (35 cm)

NICOTIANA 'LIME GREEN'

Pelargonium cultivars
Geranium

These tender perennials are probably the most familiar of all bedding plants and suit all types of containers. Pelargoniums are drought-resistant and prefer full sun. Bedding varieties have rounded, scalloped and globe-shaped heads of brightly colored flowers on long stalks. The foliage may be attractively variegated (try 'Frank Headley' or 'Robert Fish'), or their flowers may have slender petals, which give a starry effect (Stellar series). Ivy-leaved pelargoniums have fleshy leaves and trailing stems set with dainty, open-faced flowers: free-flowering, Continental-style 'Balcon' and 'Ville de Paris' varieties are popular. Plant out in spring after frosts have past. Deadhead regularly to prolong flowering.
HEIGHT: 6–12 in (15–30 cm)

POPULAR CONTAINER PLANTS

***Petunia* cultivars**
Petunia
A tender perennial bearing large, trumpet-shaped, velvety flowers, with a scent of honey. Upright varieties are suitable for troughs and window boxes, while the semi-trailing types are popular in hanging baskets. Grandiflora cultivars have large blooms and are best kept in a sheltered site, to avoid damage in heavy rain; one exception is 'Lavender Storm', which is wet-weather resistant. Multiflora types, such as the Resisto series, have small flowers that are produced in large quantities; these flowers are more resistant to rain damage. Recent introductions include Milliflora petunias, with a mass of small flowers; 'Million Bells' has unusual bell-shaped blooms with contrasting-colored throats referred to as "halos"; the Surfinia series (Grandiflora) is vigorous and very free-flowering, with a strong trailing habit. Choose a sunny site for planting, with shelter from strong winds. Deadhead regularly to prolong the season, from late spring to late fall.
HEIGHT/SPREAD: to 18 in (to 45 cm)

***Rudbeckia* 'Toto'**
Coneflower
Rudbeckias are most familiar as tall border plants, but this half-hardy annual is very compact and ideal for growing in tubs. Its daisylike flowers are rich gold, with a prominent brown central "cone." 'Toto' is free-flowering over a long season, and lasts throughout the summer until the first frosts. Flowers have good weather resistance.
HEIGHT: 10 in (25 cm)

Sanvitalia procumbens
Creeping zinnia
This half-hardy annual produces bright yellow to orange flowers with distinctive black centers. The dainty yellow daisies of 'Little Sun' show up well against a background of bronzy foliage on trailing stems. Creeping zinnias are ideal for hanging baskets and are also useful for growing in patio containers and troughs. The flowering season lasts into the fall until stopped by first frosts. Plant in full sun.
HEIGHT: to 10 in (to 25 cm)

PETUNIA 'MILLION BELLS'

Scaevola aemula
Fairy fan flower
A tender perennial with a vigorous trailing habit, which produces strong stems clothed with dark, bronzy green leaves. The flowers are very freely carried and are usually colored deep purple with a white eye. All five petals are carried on one side to give a distinctive fan shape. Popular varieties include 'New Wonder', 'Blue Shamrock', the compact 'Saphira', and white-flowered 'White Charm'. A good choice for all containers, especially hanging baskets.
HEIGHT/SPREAD: 1 ft (30 cm)

2

2

POPULAR CONTAINER PLANTS

Sutera cordata
Bacopa
A very vigorous, branching or trailing tender perennial with neat, rounded leaves and small flowers produced in great profusion. The original variety 'Snowflake' has been superceded by the trailing 'Blizzard', with relatively large white flowers. 'Knysa Hills' is an upright growing variety with pale purple flowers; 'Sea Mist' and 'Pink Domino' are trailers with pale lilac blooms. 'African Sunset' has red flowers, each with a yellow eye. Choose a sunny position. Protect from frosts.
HEIGHT/SPREAD: 16 in (40 cm)

Tropaeolum
Nasturtium
These hardy annuals are easy to grow and ideal for novice gardeners. Nasturtiums may be trailing or more bushy and are suitable for all types of containers. The edible, rounded leaves are light green (marbled white in the Alaska series) and the spurred flowers are red, yellow, salmon, or orange. Double-flowered varieties include *Tropaeolum majus* 'Darjeeling Gold' and *T. m.* 'Hermine Grashoff'. Plants are easily raised from seed sown in spring. Aphids may need to be controlled.
HEIGHT/SPREAD: 12 in (30 cm) or more

Verbena x *hybrida* **cultivars**
Verbena
Verbenas are tender perennials with pointed, bright green, tacky-textured leaves topped with heads of brightly colored flowers, often with a white eye and sometimes bicolored. Stems are lax and semi-trailing or trailing, making the plants useful for all types of containers. Bush varieties include 'Blue Lagoon' with deep blue flowers and 'Peaches and Cream' in shades of coral, yellow, and pink. Trailing varieties include the fragrant 'Pink Parfait', with pale pink and red flowers; 'Aphrodite' bearing deep purple flowers striped with white; and 'Tapien Pink' and 'Tapien Violet', both extremely free-flowering selections. Bush types can be raised from seed and planted out after frosts. Trailing types are best obtained as bedding plants. Avoid overcrowding in the container to prevent damage by mildew.
HEIGHT/SPREAD: 12 in (30 cm)

TRAILING NASTURTIUMS

Planting and growing

PLANTING AND GROWING

A plant in a container is almost entirely dependent on the gardener for its well-being – far more so than a plant growing out in the open ground in a flowerbed or border. No matter what type of container is being used, there are certain watchpoints that must be observed if container plants are to thrive and give of their best. Ample drainage, regular watering, and supplementary feeding are the foundations of good plant care. Subsequent training, pruning, and repotting as and when required will ensure that long-term plants become well established and thrive in their container garden.

3

As well as the routine, day-to-day care of plants, you need to know what steps to take if problems develop and be able to identify the cause, rectify the problem, and prevent any further damage or repeat occurrences as soon as possible. And when a plant has performed really well, it is rewarding to be able to propagate it for future years, or to supply plants for friends and neighbors.

WATER AND DRAINAGE

C ertain growing techniques apply to all container plants, whether they are in patio tubs, window boxes, or in hanging baskets. Knowing when to add water and when to stop to ensure the right balance for healthy looking plants is the way to overcome a problem that is common to all container gardens.

3

DRAINAGE HOLES

Plants in containers often swing between having too little water for their needs and far too much. Both states can be fatal. In order to prevent waterlogging, containers must provide free drainage; there should be sufficient holes in the base of the container to allow excess water to drain away. The holes are often all round the edge of the base, but clay and ceramic pots usually have a single, large, central hole.

If there are not enough drainage holes present, they can be added. In wooden, fiberglass, and plastic pots, an electric or hand drill fitted with a fairly large bit will quickly puncture holes of a useful size. A heated metal skewer held with an oven glove or thick cloth is just as effective for making holes in the base of most plastic containers.

Rather than risk damaging fragile pots without drainage holes, use the container as an outer cover for a plain pot with drainage holes, which should stand on a deep layer of grit or stones in the base. Lift out the inner pot occasionally to empty any excess water that has collected in the base of the nondraining container.

KEEPING THE FLOW

The presence of holes is not sufficient drainage on its own, because the flow of water through them can easily be impeded. Large drainage holes should be covered with a piece of narrow-gauge wire mesh to prevent the soil mix from washing through them. In all containers, a layer of coarse material at the base

TERRA-COTTA POT ON FEET

Pot feet
ensure good
drainage

SELECTION OF CERAMIC POT FEET

of the pot will allow excess water to percolate through. Concave pieces of broken clay pots (crocks) are excellent for the base layer, expecially over large drainage holes. For large containers, bulky rubble or stones should follow the broken pots; in smaller containers, use coarse gravel, grit, or similar material.

If the container is standing flush on a flat surface, water may not be able to get away from the drainage holes sufficiently well. Raise the container off the ground slightly, setting it on blocks of wood or bricks. A more attractive option is to use "pot feet" made from clay or terra-cotta, which will do the same job.

3

GRIT

RETAINING WATER

Keeping container gardens supplied with sufficient water can present just as much of a problem as making sure that they do not suffer from having too much water. Use a container that is large enough for the plant to produce a reasonable amount of growth before its roots fill all the available space, and avoid very shallow containers for deep-rooting plants. Using a soil mix that retains moisture well will cut down the amount of watering required; water-retaining granules added into the soil mix are very efficient, as each granule is able to store up to 400 times its own weight of water (see p. 52).

WATER-RETAINING GRANULES

CONTAINER SOILS

Although it is possible to use garden soil to fill containers, proprietary soil mixes will nearly always give better results. They are sterile, and unlike garden soil, they do not contain weeds, weed seeds, pests, or diseases; they also usually have a better physical structure to allow good drainage.

SOIL MIX TYPES

Proprietary brands of soil mix are either soil based or soilless.

■ **Soil-based mixes** Made from loam (rotted down meadow turf), soil-based mixes, such as multipurpose types, look and feel like fine garden soil. They retain water well, contain a long-lasting supply of plant nutrients, and are very stable when used in containers. On the downside, they are heavy and awkward to handle in bulk and messy to work with. In containers, they are most appropriate for long-term plants such as trees and shrubs.

MULTIPURPOSE SOIL-BASED MIX

■ **Soilless mixes** Based on peat or peat substitutes, such as coconut fiber, shredded bark, and sewage sludge, soilless mixes are clean, lightweight, and pleasant to handle. They contain low levels of nutrients, so plants need supplementary feeding quite soon after planting; they drain freely but also dry out quickly. Soilless mixes are suitable for nearly all types of container-grown plants, but particularly for short-term subjects such as annuals and bedding. On the downside, their light weight makes them less suitable for very tall plants that tend to become top heavy and topple over.

PEAT-FREE SOILLESS MIX

SPECIAL-PURPOSE SOILS

Ericaceous soil mix is suitable for lime-hating plants such as camellias; hanging basket soil mix is formulated to retain water well, with a long-lasting nutrient supply. Soil mixes with added insecticides protect plants against soil-borne pests, and free-draining, low-nutrient mixes provide an ideal medium for raising plants from seeds and cuttings.

SEED AND CUTTING SOIL MIX

3

PLANTING UP

When you plant up your containers, you are providing the plants with their only home for the rest of the season – so it is important that you get the planting technique right. Once you have understood the basic needs of plants and know how to provide them, planting up becomes a simple and straightforward procedure.

WHAT YOU NEED

Gather together everything you will need before you start planting. Your basic equipment should include:

■ **Trowel** Wide-bladed trowels make good-sized planting holes for bulbs and small bedding plants. Narrow-bladed versions are more practical when planting in confined spaces.

■ **Hand fork** A hand fork is useful for loosening the soil when removing weeds and when repotting a plant.

■ **Dibble** Available in a range of sizes, dibbles are used to make planting holes. Small ones are ideal for cuttings and seedlings; large ones for planting bulbs.

■ **Container** Make sure that the style of container suits the growing needs of your plants and rinse it clean before planting up.

■ **Drainage material** To prevent waterlogging, use pieces of broken clay pots or coarse gravel (see p. 45).

■ **Water-retaining granules** Refer to the manufacturer's guidelines to assess the correct amount for your container (see p. 52).

■ **Soil mix** Choose a soil mix that is appropriate to your plant's growing needs (see p. 46).

■ **Plants** Use healthy plants that are large enough to be handled comfortably (see pp. 48–49).

■ **Watering can** Make sure that your can is a manageable size, especially if you need to lift it to reach hanging baskets and wall mangers. A long spout will allow you to reach plants.

3

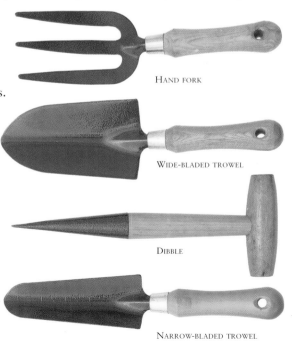

HAND FORK

WIDE-BLADED TROWEL

DIBBLE

NARROW-BLADED TROWEL

BUYING PLANTS

There is no shortage of outlets selling suitable plants to grow in containers, especially in spring, when it seems almost every shop has a display of bedding plants. For some of the more unusual plants, however, a little more advance planning is required. There are three main ways to buy plants.

WHERE TO BUY

■ **Garden centers** Specialist nurseries are perhaps the most popular places for gardeners to buy container plants. They usually offer a good choice of plant types and varieties, and you are able to make your own selection. Staff are likely to be knowledgeable and the plants should be well looked after – although this is variable.

■ **Nonspecialist retailers** Market stalls, private sellers, and hardware and chain stores often sell more popular types of plants, although their quality may be rather poor as staff usually have no special training in plant care. However, prices are likely to be very competitive, and you can see what you are buying.

■ **Mail order** Probably the largest range of varieties, including new and unusual types, is available from specialist mail-order outlets. Many seed companies, as well as specialist nurseries, supply young plants in the spring. Orders have to be made several weeks in advance of the plants being needed, and shipping costs will add to the overall price. The quality of the plants cannot be seen until they arrive, but most reputable firms will replace damaged or substandard stock.

TYPES OF PLANTS

Plants are sold at different stages of growth, from tiny seedlings that will need transplanting into pots and hardening off before going outdoors to pot-ready plants that are ready to be planted out immediately. The type of plant that you choose will depend on your time and budget.

Healthy buds indicate good plant growth

SUN OR CAPE DAISY
(*OSTEOSPERMUM*)

3

■ **Seedlings** The least expensive way of buying seedlings is an open tray, although the seedlings in them are not as easy to transplant. Open trays of seedling plants need to be transferred to compartments within larger trays or individual pots of soil mix and grown for several weeks. You will need a suitable light, frost-free place in which to grow the seedlings, as well as spare pots or trays, soil mix, and the time for transplanting.

TRAY PLANTS

3

Damage-free foliage indicates good health

■ **Plug plants** Available in a wide range of sizes, plug plants are grown individually in small cells of soil mix in a molded tray. Plug plants are larger and sturdier than seedlings and each have their own, firm rootball. They usually need to be potted up for growing before they can be planted out, but otherwise they are easier and less time-consuming to look after than seedlings.

POT-READY PLANT

■ **Tray plants** Older seedlings are often sold divided into compartmented trays to give them extra room to grow into sturdy young plants. They are not quite as easy to transplant as plug plants because they are likely to suffer more root disturbance, but they are generally less expensive. You will usually need to have facilities to harden off the plants before setting them outside.

■ **Pot-ready plants** Although more expensive, large plug plants or plants that have been grown on in individual pots will be ready for planting at the time of purchase. Some may need to be hardened off before planting outside.

PROPAGATION

If you have the space and equipment, you might like to try raising your own stock of plants to fill your containers. A frost-free greenhouse is the ideal environment for propagating, but a warm conservatory or a bright window sill will also serve the purpose.

GROWING FROM SEED

■ **Tray preparation** Fill a seed tray with seed and cuttings soil mix, level it and firm the surface with a wooden presser. Water the soil mix using a can fitted with a fine rose.

■ **Sowing** Sprinkle the seed thinly over the surface of the soil, and cover it lightly with a thin, even layer of soil mix or silver sand. Cover with a propagator hood or another seed tray turned upside down.

■ **Cultivation** Leave the seed tray in an evenly warm place, and mist well whenever the surface looks as though it is drying out. As soon as the first few seedlings are showing through, make sure that the tray is kept in bright but diffused light. When the seedlings are large enough to handle, separate them out into another tray or individual pots to give them more growing room. Always handle them by their first pair of leaves, never by their stems.

CLOCHES
Cloches provide young plants and seedlings that need to be hardened off with additional protection against the cold. They also shield tender young leaves from attack by birds and slugs. Readymade cloches are available in a range of sizes, suitable for covering individual plants or seed trays. The more expensive models are made from glass, which is the traditional material, but transparent plastic is just as effective and less prone to breakage. Homemade versions can be fashioned from wire hoops and horticultural film or, simpler still, from a transparent plastic bottle cut in half and placed over an individual plant.

3

SOWING SEED

Allow even spacing
between seeds

TAKING CUTTINGS

If you find that a cultivar does not come true from seed, or if it is not possible to increase a plant by division, then taking cuttings is your best solution. Cuttings can be taken at anytime during the growing season and should produce root systems within two to three weeks of cultivation.

1 Select a strong-growing, healthy, preferably non-flowering shoot and cut it off just above a node (where the leaves join the stem). Trim the cutting so that it has about four pairs of leaves, cutting just below a node and removing the bottom pair of leaves cleanly.

Use a clean, sharp blade

3

Insert cuttings evenly around the edge

2 Insert the cutting into a pot of moist seed and cutting soil mix topped with a layer of silver sand, and firm it in well. Cover with a propagator hood to maintain a humid atmosphere and water regularly to keep the soil moist. Leave the pot in light shade until roots have formed and the cutting starts to grow away at the tip.

ROUTINE CARE

Whether your containers are planted up with short-term summer displays or long-term shrubs and specimen trees, they will need regular attention and maintenance, especially during the growing season, to ensure a prolonged period of interest and pleasure.

WATERING

Perhaps the most time-consuming task associated with container gardening is watering, with demand reaching its peak during the flowering season, especially if you have densely planted containers. Most containers will need watering daily in summer, and some may need to be refreshed two or three times a day. The need for water is greatest in hot, dry weather, but even when it rains, the dense leaf cover over the surface of the soil will probably mean that little rain water penetrates the soil mix to any depth.

A well-balanced watering can with a long spout is useful for reaching hanging baskets and wall pots, but if you have lots of containers to look after, a hose is much quicker. Fit it with a long lance that can be turned on and off at the end farthest from the tap. If you are unable to spend much time on watering your plants regularly, you can set up an automatic drip or trickle watering system, which is controlled by a fully adjustable computer fitted to the tap.

Water-retaining granules, which look like grains of sugar when dry (see p. 45), can absorb many times their own weight in water. If they are distributed through the soil mix, they retain water that would otherwise drain away, making it available to the plants. Mix a small quantity of granules with the soil mix when planting up and it will cut down the subsequent need for watering considerably.

Long spout allows access to high wall pots and hanging baskets

LONG-SPOUTED
WATERING CAN

3

FEEDING

In densely planted containers, plants compete for nutrients from the soil. Soil-based mixes are able to keep plants supplied with food for a while, but soilless mixes may need supplementary feeding soon after planting. One or two specialist soil mixes are also available (see p. 46).

Fertilizers contain the major plant nutrients of nitrogen, potassium, and phosphorus, as well as other minor nutrients. For flourishing foliage, choose a nitrogen-rich fertilizer; for good flowering, opt for one that is high in potassium. Fertilizers are available as granules, powders, or liquids. One of the most useful forms is slow-release granules or feedsticks: added to the soil mix at the start of the season, these release their nutrients gradually, sometimes lasting all season long. Powders and liquids are usually diluted and applied with a watering can; they are quick acting, and often weak solutions can be applied at every watering. The fastest results are produced by foliar feeds, which are taken up by the plants' leaves; they help to reduce nutrient deficiencies and act as a general "pick-me-up" for plants under stress. They can be very useful for supplying nutrients to lime-hating plants that are not in their ideal soil conditions.

3

LIQUID FERTILIZER

Warning

When applying any fertilizer, always follow the application instructions on the package, and remember that too much food can be just as damaging to a plant as can too little food.

POWDER FERTILIZER

FERTILIZER FEEDSTICKS

PLANT SUPPORTS

The necessity for plant supports depends
upon the size and type of plant being
grown and the position of the
container – whether it is in a windy
or sheltered place.

Climbing plants, unless they are
grown as trailers, need a framework
on which to grow. This can be
provided by a section of wooden
or plastic trellis, either fixed in the
container or attached to a nearby
wall. If the plant is tall and leafy, the
depth of soil in the pot may not be
sufficient to support it, and the trellis is
then best fixed to a firm base outside the
container. A wigwam constructed from bamboo
canes placed around the edge of the container
and tied together at their tips is also effective.

The stems of bushy and shrubby plants may
need individual supports to maintain their shape.
Dark green split canes are less obvious when set
among the branches and tied to individual stems.

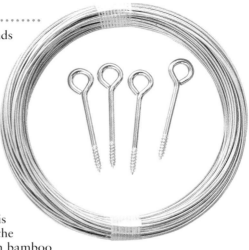

HORTICULTURAL WIRE
AND VINE EYES

3

Ring prevents chafing
between stake and trunk

TREE STRAP AND STAKE

Grille holds tall
flowering stems
in place

RING CANE SUPPORT

SELECTION
OF CANES
AND PLASTIC
TIE RINGS

KEEPING IN TRIM

Container-grown trees and shrubs and perennial climbers are most likely to need pruning; this may be to keep them to an attractive shape, to encourage flowering or to restrict them to a practical size. Use sharp pruning shears and make cuts just above a bud. Always remove damaged, dead, or diseased wood completely, whenever it is seen; otherwise, the timing and type of pruning depends on the individual plant.

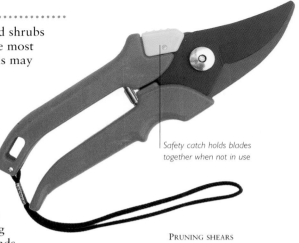

Safety catch holds blades together when not in use

PRUNING SHEARS

Deadheading is a form of pruning that can be carried out to advantage on nearly all container plants. As well as making the plant look tidier by removing faded flowers, if it is done early enough it will prevent energy being wasted in seed production and stimulate further flowering throughout the season. Faded flowers can be pinched off with the fingers or removed with shears, cutting the stem down to a leaf joint or removing it completely.

3

Warning

Hands need to be protected by gardening gloves when carrying out routine tasks in the garden. Choose heavy duty gauntlets when pruning thorny stems and brambles; use lightweight cotton gloves when weeding and deadheading.

REPOTTING

Perennial plants, including trees and shrubs, will need occasional repotting to ensure healthy growth.

■ **Repotting in a new pot** Once a young plant has filled its pot with roots, it should be repotted into a larger pot. Water it well an hour or two before removing it from the pot. Stand the plant on a layer of fresh soil mix in a new pot that is one or two sizes larger. Backfill around the rootball with more soil mix, pushing the soil down well, until it just covers the old surface. Water well.

■ **Repotting with new soil** Once a plant has reached as large a size pot as it requires, it can be repotted in the same pot. Remove it as before and crumble away some of the old soil mix from the outside of the rootball. Tease out any constricted roots; some of these can be pruned back carefully if you want to restrict the plant's size. Mix some fresh soil mix with slow-release fertilizer granules and place a layer of this in the original pot. Return the plant to the pot, filling in down the sides with more soil mix. Water well.

PROBLEM SOLVING

Like all living things, plants are prone to their share of problems. Pests and diseases are always the chief suspects, but there may be a whole range of other causes such as inappropriate feeding and watering, poor soil, or weather damage. An accurate identification of the trouble is an essential first step toward putting things right.

CULTURAL PROBLEMS

When things go wrong with plants, pests and diseases tend to get the blame, but it may well be a cultural fault that is causing the problem.

■ **Nutrient deficiencies** These show up as yellowing foliage, or leaves with marked yellow patches or yellow veins; a fertilizer containing trace elements will usually cure these.

■ **Wilting foliage and stems** This may be caused by lack of water at the roots, or even waterlogged soil.

■ **Stunted growth** This may be due to sudden cold or windy conditions, or lack of nutrients in the soil mix.

■ **Leaf scorch** Strong sun can cause leaves to blotch and shrivel.

COMMON PESTS AND DISEASES

Good observational skills are the key to coping with pest and disease attacks; if an infestation is spotted at an early stage, it is much easier to deal with than when it has become well established. Look particularly at the growing points of plants and check the undersides of leaves, as symptoms may first show themselves here.

• **Slugs** Have voracious appetites for tender foliage and can reduce susceptible plants such as hostas to skeletons almost overnight. Remove slugs by handpicking them after dark; or use beer traps, proprietary organic controls, or slug pellets containing metaldehyde or methiocarb.

• **Caterpillars** Chew holes and ragged pieces out of leaves and shoots. Remove caterpillars by handpicking or by spraying with derris or bifenthrin.

• **Aphids** Colonize growing tips, shoots, and buds of plants in vast numbers. They can distort and stunt growth and may spread viral diseases. In the early stages of an attack, aphids can be washed away from affected shoots with soapy water. Chemical controls include pirimicarb, bifenthrin, derris, and horticultural soap.

• **Powdery mildew** Powdery white patches on plant foliage; most common in hot, dry weather and often caused by overcrowding plants in one area. Treat outbreaks with a fungicide such as carbendazim.

• **Rusts** Pale spots on the leaf surface with brown or orange powdery spores on the underside. Leaves fall early and growth is stunted. Remove and burn affected leaves; spray with a fungicide such as propiconazole.

HOLIDAY CARE

To keep your container plants well watered while you are away from home, group them together and set up an automated sprinkler or drip system; this need not be too costly and can be very effective. Always test the system in advance and ask a friend or neighbor to check that it is working while you are away. Just before you leave, prune back bedding plants and tender perennials; this will encourage new growth and produce a flush of flowers for your return.

TAKING SHELTER
A neighbor will find it easier to water and care for your plants if you group your containers together in a sheltered, lightly shaded spot.

3

OUT-OF-SEASON INTEREST

Containers come into their own in summer when they are filled with an abundance of colorful flowers, but there is no need to store them away when the first frost arrives. Plants in containers can brighten up gardens and window sills right through fall and winter and into spring, when they are often even more welcome than in summer.

MAINTAINING INTEREST

■ **Fall** Perennials such as Kaffir lilies *(Schizostylis coccinea)* and michaelmas daisies help to continue the summer's flowers into fall, and are followed by fall-flowering bulbs like nerines, colchicums, and cyclamen. Brilliant fall foliage colors are provided by Japanese maples and witch hazels, while glossy orange-red berries from firethorn and cotoneaster develop their rich red tints.

■ **Winter** Delicate flowers are provided by laurustinus *(Viburnum tinus)*, witch hazel, winter iris, and the sweet-scented shrubby honeysuckles. The bold colors of winter-flowering pansies and the more subtle shades of heathers, such as *Erica carnea* varieties, are ideal for growing in window boxes, wall pots, and other small containers. Bright, glowing foliage from golden-variegated ivies, euonymus, and *Eleagnus* compensates for the lack of sun on a dull winter day.

■ **Spring** Snowdrops and the earliest crocuses and miniature narcissi help to ease the transition between winter and spring. As the days lengthen, myriad other bulbs come into flower,

accompanied by primulas and polyanthus, double daisies, and a renewed flush of winter pansies. Several varieties of heather *(Calluna)* bear beautifully colored foliage tips in spring, and hellebores carry their nodding heads of green, purple, or white cupshaped flowers.

BERRY BRIGHT
The blazing-orange berries of firethorn provide a splash of color in the fall garden once the last of the summer flowers have died down.

3

Pots, tubs, and troughs

4

POTS, TUBS, AND TROUGHS

Freestanding pots, patio tubs, and troughs are perhaps the most popular types of container. Planted with spring-flowering bulbs, summer blooms, or winter foliage, they can be moved around the garden to give an attractive display throughout the year.

Whether they are filled with flowers and displayed in a grouping or planted up with a single specimen, perhaps trained as a standard and used as a focal point, containers are infinitely versatile. Even an old sink, bathtub, or half-barrel can be transformed into an object of beauty when incorporated into a themed planting or used as a novelty container for a water garden – the possibilities are endless.

4

POSITIONING POTS

Freestanding containers are valued for their versatility. Ornamental pots can be used to make bold statements in a garden; large tubs can be moved to form a temporary screen, while oversized troughs and urns are ideal for accommodating large specimen plants, or for cramming full with long-lasting displays of colorful annuals.

MOVING CONTAINERS

One of the advantages of freestanding containers, such as pots, tubs, and troughs, is that they can be moved around the garden. This means that they can be brought into a prominent position when the plants they contain are at their best, and then moved to somewhere less obvious when their main display is over.

Some containers are very heavy, and moving them around the garden is not a job to be undertaken lightly.

TIMBER TUB

PEDESTAL BOWL

Try to place any heavy, awkward containers in their final positions before planting, as the weight of damp soil once they are filled may make it almost impossible to move them. If you move your containers regularly, it might be worth your while investing in a small, purpose-made trolley on casters; these are generally available from large garden equipment suppliers.

Lightweight containers are quite easy to move about, although even with these, you should not underestimate the weight of soil once they are planted up.

In order to drain freely, pots should be slightly raised from the ground; three or four small blocks of wood or purpose-made pot feet do the job well. Make sure the pot is stable on these blocks, as delicate pots can easily be damaged or broken if they are knocked over.

4

CHANGING THE LEVEL

Pots and tubs do not all have to be displayed at ground level; raising them helps to give height to a garden and allows a well-planted container to be more easily admired, perhaps forming a focal point. It also allows trailing plants to fall gracefully, extending below the base of the container. Garden walls, raised beds, flights of steps, and purpose-made plinths and pedestals offer suitable places for raised pots.

It is important to ensure that a raised pot is fixed securely; if it falls, there is not only the risk of damage to the pot, but of human injury.

■ **Walls** A flat, level coping stone on the top of a wall enables a pot to be positioned centrally and reasonably safely; on walls extending above

BATH TIME BLUES
A decorated metal trough provides ample room for this *Hydrangea macrophylla* bearing large blue mopheads of flowers.

> ### Warning
>
> Containers set on pedestals or tall pillars can be particularly dangerous, especially if there are children in the garden who may pull the container on top of them. To reduce the risk of accidents, cement the container firmly to the top of the pedestal, or use an all-in-one arrangement whereby the container is constructed as an integral part of the pedestal.

head height, extra measures are advisable. Hold troughs in place with an L-shaped metal bracket, set railings along the edge of the wall to act as restraints, or simply cement the container into place.

■ **Steps** Pots should be placed well to the sides of flights of steps so that they do not impede access. Trim back trailing or spreading plants regularly to ensure that their foliage does not present a hazard to passersby.

4

GENERAL CARE

The shape of a container plays an important part in the amount of care it needs once planted. If the surface area of the soil is large in proportion to its volume, the soil will dry out more quickly. Shallow bowls and troughs have a large surface area, and therefore need much more frequent watering than a deep pot.

MATERIALS

The material a container is made from will also have an effect on plant growth. Porous materials like terra-cotta lose water by evaporation; they can also draw moisture out of the soil when first filled and planted up. Glazed or plastic containers are nonporous and need less watering, but they are more likely to become waterlogged. Where items have been adapted to become plant containers rather than being purpose made, they may need special treatment before planting. A coating of bitumen-based paint will seal the inside of a wooden or metal container, helping to prevent rot and rust as well as protecting the plants from the presence of damaging chemicals. A plastic liner can be used instead of bitumen-based paint, but it is important to ensure that the base of the polyethylene is well punctured to allow water to drain away.

PREPARED HALF-BARREL

ROUTINE CHECKS

■ **Roots** When growing trees, shrubs, and perennials in containers, check the base of the pot regularly. Roots emerging through the drainage holes indicate that the plant is ready for repotting (see p. 55). If the pot is left standing on open ground, the roots will penetrate down into the soil; when the pot is eventually lifted, these roots will be damaged or destroyed and the plant's growth could be severely checked.

MAKING A SINK GARDEN

Stone troughs can be expensive and difficult to obtain. A good substitute can be made from a glazed kitchen sink covered in hypertufa, which is a mixture of peat and cement.

• Clean the sink and coat the outside in a bonding agent; leave it to dry.

• Mix equal parts of peat or peat substitute with coarse sand and cement; add water to give a suitable consistency for coating the sink.

• With gloved hands, apply a ¾-in (2-cm) layer of hypertufa to the sink.

• Leave the sink to dry for several days, then roughen the dry surface with a wire brush to achieve a stone-textured finish. Add moss and lichen to complete the effect.

4

4

■ **Moisture** Water your containers regularly; if too much moisture is lost, the soil will dry out and shrink away from the sides of the pot. Any subsequent watering will pass down the gully between soil and pot, rather than soaking through the soil. Stand the container on a gravel-filled saucer to prevent drying out (but do not leave the base of the pot standing in

SHELTERED IN SHADE
This cool, shady corner provides welcome shelter from bright midday sun, which can scorch foliage and deprive roots of much-needed moisture.

water at anytime) or add a layer of gravel over the surface of the soil. This mulch helps to retain moisture and usually sets the plants off well.

PLANTING A POT

Your first attempt at planting up a container can often be a little daunting. Gather together a couple of inspirational pictures to use as reference and make sure that you have everything that you need at hand before you start; then simply follow the steps below.

A POTTED POSY

1 Rinse out the container with water then place some broken pieces of clay pot (crocks) directly over the drainage hole. Add a layer of coarse gravel, grit, or small stones to the base of the pot to ensure that the soil can drain freely. If the container has small holes round the edge of the base rather than a single, large, central drainage hole, the layer of stones or gravel will be sufficient on its own.

Sprinkle water-retaining granules evenly through soil mix

4

2 Fill the pot three-quarters full with soil-based or soilless mix; the latter tends to be the most popular because it is lightweight and clean (see p. 46). When using soilless mix, it is a good idea to add some slow-release fertilizer and water-retaining granules at this point; follow the manufacturer's instructions to assess the correct quantity. Sprinkle the supplements over the soil and mix them in by hand.

3 Top up the pot with soil mix to just below the brim. Keeping the plants in their pots, set them out on the surface of the soil until you are satisfied with the overall appearance. Start with a tall, upright plant in the center, then place lower-growing, bushy plants around it, and add some trailers at the edge of the pot. Keep an even balance of plants around the pot, if the arrangement is going to be viewed from all sides.

4 Remove the central plant from its pot by turning it upside down, holding the stem between your fingers, and tapping the rim sharply; the rootball should slide out cleanly.

5 Make a hole in the soil and insert the plant so that the top of the rootball is just covered with fresh soil. Firm it lightly into position. Treat the rest of the plants in the same way.

Balanced all-round display of flowers

6 Once the planting is complete, water the finished pot overhead with a fine rose on the can. As well as settling the plants into place, this will freshen them up, washing off any traces of soil mix from the leaves and flowers. Check the moisture content of the soil after a couple of hours if water-retaining granules have been used – it may need a further watering once the granules have absorbed moisture.

4

A POT FOR WINTER

Containers for winter interest tend to rely mainly on foliage plants, but there are some flowers available that will help to brighten up dull winter days. The Universal series of winter-flowering pansies produce their best blooms during late fall, but in a fairly sheltered position they will continue to flower through the winter until they have a further large flush of blooms in early spring. Winter-flowering heathers are another good choice; varieties of *Erica carnea* are available in a wide range of shades and are undeterred by the weather.

FROST AND SNOW

A simple arrangement of green and white is particularly suitable for winter days, adding brightness but with a suggestion of frost and snow. *Euonymus fortunei* 'Harlequin' is a new variety of compact growth, its foliage heavily mottled and splashed with brilliant white; the white-margined *E. f.* 'Silver Queen' could be used as a substitute. *Erica carnea* 'Springwood White' is a favorite and reliable winter-flowering heather variety. It makes a vigorous plant with bright green foliage and a mass of white flowers, each bloom tipped with rusty brown. The rambling stems of *Vinca minor* carry neat, oval, glossy, dark green leaves. In late winter or early spring, the form *V. m.* f. *alba* bears white periwinkle flowers that tone perfectly with the white and green theme.

4

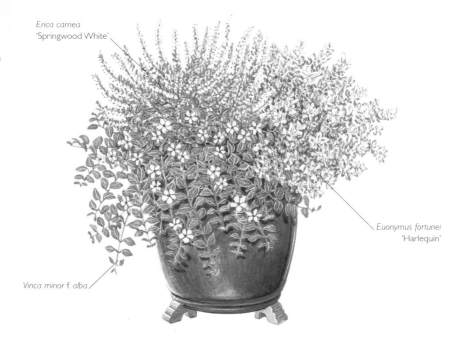

Erica carnea
'Springwood White'

Euonymus fortunei
'Harlequin'

Vinca minor f. alba

SPRING SUNSHINE

Many winter-flowering plants redouble their efforts as spring arrives, but there is also a good range of spring bedding plants and spring-flowering bulbs to provide instant color. Most bedding plants should be able to withstand light frost but they will need to be hardened off before being set outdoors permanently.

TOUCH OF SUNLIGHT

The bright golden color scheme of this container display brings a touch of sunlight to the garden just as it emerges from winter. The most prominent plant is the *Ranunculus asiaticus* Turban Group, with heavily ruffled flowers of soft yellow-orange laced with deeper color on the edges of the petals. The deeply cut, fresh green foliage is also attractive. Yellow and white primroses produce prolonged flushes of bloom; the white-flowered form has a deep yellow eye that picks up the color of the ranunculus. *Tulipa* 'Glück' is one of the Kauffmaniana group, with streaked and mottled foliage; the elegantly shaped flowers have creamy yellow petals with a central stripe of rusty orange-red. Curling around the pot are tendrils of *Hedera helix* 'Yellow Ripple', a variety of ivy with attractively shaped, variegated deep yellow and light green leaves.

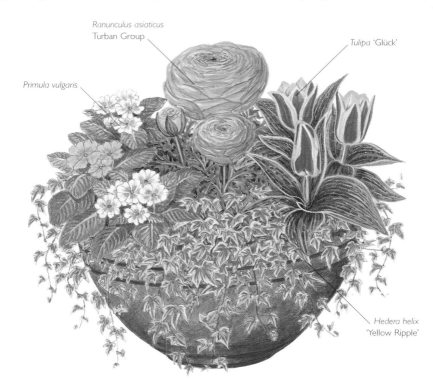

Ranunculus asiaticus
Turban Group

Tulipa 'Glück'

Primula vulgaris

Hedera helix
'Yellow Ripple'

4

SUMMERTIME PLEASURES

I n summer, there is almost an embarrassment of choices for the
container gardener. This is the peak season for pots, tubs, and
troughs; wherever you look there are containers spilling over with
a mass of color from a vast range of flowering plants.

COOL AND LIGHT

Many containers are planted up
without a great deal of thought or
planning. The ensuing "riot of color"
may be just what is wanted, but
a more careful selection of shade
can often give far more effective
results. The "hot" colors – red,
orange, and bright yellow – are lively,
vibrant, and instantly attract the eye.
In contrast, "cool" colors – blue,
white, and green – are more restful
and appear more distant and less
obtrusive. Container gardens may
be planned on a theme of either hot
or cool shades, depending upon the
effect you want to create, but in
each case a small touch of contrast
helps to intensify their effect.

In the wooden trough illustrated,
the main tones used are cool and
light. The trailing stems of golden
creeping Jenny (*Lysimachia
nummularia* 'Aurea') are studded
with round leaves of a sharp citrus-
green shade; the flowers of the
tobacco plant (*Nicotiana* 'Lime
Green') produce a soft haze of palest
green above the deep green foliage.
Dotted in among them, the relatively
few brilliant red blooms of *Nicotiana*
'Domino Red' are given maximum
impact by their sharp contrast with
the cool tones surrounding them.

In the same way, a planting of
bright reds, oranges, and intense,
deep yellows can be thrown into
more effective relief by the addition
of some cooler shades – a silver-
foliaged plant such as *Helichrysum
petiolare* is an excellent choice.

4

Lysimachia
nummularia 'Aurea'

Nicotiana 'Domino Red'

Nicotiana 'Lime Green'

PINKS AND PASTELS

Different shades of pink and pastels
feature in the illustrated tub,
which teams a weeping standard
rose (here, *Rosa* 'Nozomi') with
garden pinks *(Dianthus)* around
the base of the plant. 'Nozomi'
makes a very attractive informal
standard, with its spreading,
slightly weeping branches
festooned in summer with
delicate shell-pink, single
flowers. The small, ferny, dark
green leaves have a bluish cast,
which is echoed by the silver-gray
foliage of *Dianthus* 'Houndspool
Ruby,' while the rich pink double
flowers complement the paler pink
of the roses.

Using a wider range of adjacent
colors gives more scope for
incorporating different plants and
varieties. Pink, salmon, magenta,
lilac, purple, and blue all harmonize
well but allow a wide range of
individual shades to form part of
the scheme, giving an impression
of a varied, multicolored container
that still retains a satisfying and
well-integrated color scheme.

A single-color planting scheme
can make a very striking container
arrangement, but needs the skill
of an experienced gardener to
successfully incorporate the green of
the plants' foliage into the scheme.
White- or golden-variegated foliage is

Rosa 'Nozomi'

Dianthus 'Houndspool Ruby'

particularly useful in helping to link
foliage into a single-color scheme;
equally, you may find a color wheel
useful when planning a planting
scheme. Reading clockwise, the
wheel colors are blue, green, yellow,
orange, red, and purple. Adjacent
colors on the wheel tone with each
other, while opposite colors contrast.
Red and green are directly opposite
each other on the wheel, giving a
strong contrast between red flowers
and green leaves, but purple, blue, or
orange flower shades can be more
difficult to work with. White makes
an effective combination with green
foliage, as does yellow which is
adjacent to green on the color wheel.

WEEPING STANDARDS

Most ramblers, lax climbers, and
trailing ground-cover roses can be
trained as weeping standards,
including: *Rosa* 'Dorothy Perkins'
(rose-pink); *R.* 'Excelsa' (crimson);
R. 'Grouse' (blush pink); and
R. 'Sander's White Rambler'.

4

HEIGHT AND TEXTURE

The overwhelming choice of colors offered by container plants, especially annuals and biennials, makes it easy to overlook other features in a container garden. For example, differently shaped flowers, from trumpets to bells, can increase variety and interest in a display. Many schemes, especially those comprising mainly low-growing bedding plants, could benefit from some additional height. Areas of dull foliage in a planting can be interspersed with more textural plants, such as spiny, soft-haired, or delicately divided leaves.

RAISING STANDARDS

The most usual way of adding height is by including one or two tall specimens in a mixed planting, or by devoting some containers entirely to tall plants that can be positioned among containers of low-growing subjects. The clear-stemmed tree shape of a trained standard also makes an ideal choice for adding height to containers because it allows additional low-level planting around its base. Standards can be formed from a wide range of plants, some of the most popular of which are flowering crab apples and cherries, roses (see p. 69), marguerites, bay (Laurus nobilis), and fuchsias. Another way of adding height is to grow climbing plants up a support. A narrow piece of trellis, a wigwam of canes, or specially made decorative wire or wooden globes or pyramids can all make effective features. Climbing or scrambling plants such as ivy, nasturtiums, clematis, honeysuckle, and black-eyed Susan (Thunbergia) are all suitable for training on supports.

HOLLY STANDARD
A holly tree grown as a standard produces an eye-catching sphere of glossy, spiny foliage, adding height to the colorful underplanting of fuchsias and trailing plants.

ADDING TEXTURE

The word "texture" is usually used to describe the feel of a substance, but while some plants are, indeed, very tactile, texture when applied to plants usually describes a visual effect. Most containers are planned around flower or foliage color and plant form, but the texture of flowers or foliage is another aspect to take into consideration. The sympathetic use of different textures can make the difference between a run-of-the-mill planting and one that has a really outstanding effect. Plant foliage may be sturdy, firm, and bold, or feathery, light, and hazy; it may be sharply pointed and swordlike or softly rounded. As a general rule, feathery plants provide a good background and margin for a container planting, with bolder shapes displayed against them. It is the finely cut or fluffy plants, such as ferns and grasses, that usually supply the contrast of texture in a mixed planting.

Texture can be introduced by means of a planting prop. A wire shape such as a pyramid or ball can be filled with soil mix held in place by sphagnum moss around the outside, and low-growing plants such as pansies, lobelia, or double daisies planted through the moss – rather like an upside-down hanging basket.

TEXTURED FOLIAGE

Alchemilla mollis
Lady's mantle
Softly scalloped, downy leaves that hold sparkling drops of dew, with open, fluffy heads of tiny lime-green flowers.

Artemisia
Wormwood
Bright steel-blue or silver foliage, often finely cut or filigreed, and sometimes aromatic. *A. schmidtiana* 'Nana' or *A.* 'Powis Castle' are good choices.

Cordyline australis
New Zealand cabbage palm
A strong palmlike outline with spiky, swordshaped foliage with bold stripes and margins. Suitable for patio tubs and conservatories.

Festuca glauca
Blue fescue, Blue grass
A fully hardy, fine-leaved evergreen bearing tufted blue-green to blue-gray grass that forms a hazy mound (see p. 23).

Gypsophila paniculata
Baby's breath
Delicate branching flower stems bearing clusters of tiny trumpetshaped flowers that form a misty white cloud.

Nigella damascena
Love-in-a-mist
Blue-petaled flowers, surrounded by a collar of green, slender leaves, arise from finely cut, bright green foliage. *N. d.* 'Dwarf Moody Blue' and *N. d.* 'Blue Midget' are dwarf varieties.

Phormium tenax
New Zealand flax
A striking rosette of bold, swordlike, sturdy leaves, in yellow-green to dark green, often striped. *P. t.* 'Bronze Baby' is a dwarf hybrid with attractive bronze leaves.

Sempervivum andrachnoideum
Cobweb houseleek
Rosettes of succulent, fleshy leaves are laced together at their tips with a cobweb of fine hairs.

Stachys byzantina
Lambs' ears
Silver-green leaves covered in silky-soft hairs that give them a velvety look and feel. Spikes of pink-purple flowers appear in summer.

4

WATER FEATURES

There is something special about a water feature in any garden. Water has a cooling, tranquil effect; it sparkles in the sunlight, attracts brilliantly colored damselflies and enables a whole new range of attractive plants to be grown. A mini-pool in a container can prove to be a very successful feature, whatever the size of your garden.

BARRELS OF FUN

Wooden barrels are the most popular choice for a water garden, but any sturdy, waterproof container of 15 in (38 cm) deep or more can be used.

■ **Preparation** Give the barrel a thorough cleaning before use. If you have doubts about how waterproof it is, the interior can be lined with butyl rubber or heavy-duty black polyethylene, or painted with a bitumen-based paint. It is best to soak the barrel before treatment to allow the staves to swell.

■ **Siting** Place the prepared container in its permanent position before filling it; choose an open, sunny spot away from overhanging trees that will drop leaf debris. Place one or two bricks in the container on which to set baskets of marginal plants, which need shallower water over their roots, then half fill with water.

■ **Planting** Arrange a selection of aquatic plants in planting baskets lined with hessian and filled with good-quality aquatic soil; top-dress the surface with a layer of gravel and lower the baskets into the water. Trickle more water into the container until it is full.

■ **Fish** One or two goldfish can be introduced to the water garden after a couple of weeks; they are useful to control mosquitoes, which will otherwise breed in the water. However, you will probably need to take them out of the pool for the winter, as the volume of water will be too small to protect them from freezing temperatures.

BRIMMING OVER
The soothing sound of gurgling water is provided by this amusing water feature made from a pumped spout and two wooden barrels.

4

CONTROLLING ALGAE

No matter how careful your preparation of a new pond, the water will turn opaque-green (or sometimes red) within a short time of filling, as millions of algae colonize the water. Algae also tend to recur from time to time in very small pools. With the correct balance of pond plants and oxygenators, the algae will eventually disappear of their own accord as the plants use up the excess minerals on which algae thrive. Resist the temptation to change the water, as this will only prolong the problem.

PLANTS FOR THE POOL

OXYGENATORS
Plant these at the bottom of the barrel where they can remain submerged.

Apium inundatum
Callitriche verna
Eleocharis acicularis
Elodea canadensis;
  E. crispa; E. densa
Fontinalis antipyretica
Hottonia palustris
Myriophyllum hipuroides;
  M. scabratum;
  M. spicatum
Potamogeton crispus

FLOATING LEAF AQUATICS
Aponogeton distachyos
Water hawthorn
Elongated, oval leaves and unusually shaped, white, scented flowers.

Nymphaea
Water lilies
Choose dwarf varieties that need a planting depth of 12 in (30 cm). Plant one waterlily per barrel.

Varieties
N. candida (white)
N. 'Ellisiana' (deep red)
N. 'Froebelii' (red)
N. odorata minor (white)

MARGINALS
Plant marginals in containers and position them so that 2–3 in (5–8 cm) of water covers the crown of the plant.

Caltha palustris
'Flore Pleno'
Marsh marigold
Compact growing, with rounded leaves and fully double yellow flowers.

Iris laevigata **'Variegata'**
Variegated water iris
Lavender-blue flowers and swordlike, cream- and green-striped leaves.

Menyanthes trifoliata
Bog bean
Spikes of white star-shaped flowers flushed pink with fringed petals. Leaves are bright green.

Pontederia cordata
Pickerel weed
Spikes of blue flowers rise in late summer from glossy green, oval leaves.

Typha minima
Miniature reedmace
Grassy foliage and small, brown, bulrushlike flower heads.

4

HAIRGRASS
(*ELEOCHARIS ACICULARIS*)

SPECIMEN PLANTS

A container planted up with a single, impressive specimen can make an excellent focal point for a garden and can be more effective than a colorful and varied mixed planting. Specimen plants should be striking in terms of their flowers and foliage but, more often, it is their overall shape that earns them the title of "architectural" plants.

MAKING A STATEMENT

Many specimen plants have a bold, imposing, even eccentric outline that needs to be offset against a plain background for maximum effect. Examples include the spiky, swordlike forms of cordylines and phormiums, the strangely twisted and contorted corkscrew hazel (*Corylus avellana*), or the bold mounds of giant feather grass.

Other plants can be trained and clipped to achieve impressive shapes. Bay laurel and box are favorite candidates for training into standards, balls, pyramids, spirals, cones, and a range of other stately forms.

FERN PALM AS
A SPECIMEN

FLOWERS AND FOLIAGE

Many shrubs, including flowering species, make excellent specimen plants when they are grown as standards: fuchsias, marguerites, roses, and hollies are popular, but willow, laurustinus, and photinia make more unusual focal points.

The delicate foliage and fall color of Japanese maples make these small trees popular to use as specimens for containers. Specimens grown for their flowers have a short but spectacular season of interest. In early spring, the perfect, waxy flowers of camellias shine richly among the dark green, glossy foliage; a few weeks later, the loosely formed

white flowers of star magnolia (*Magnolia stellata*) deck the bare, spreading branches. Angels' trumpets (*Brugmansia* x *candida* 'Knightii') make a rounded shrub with impressive leaves, and beautiful, trumpetshaped flowers that release their perfume on summer evenings.

ARCHITECTURAL PLANTS

Acer palmatum
Japanese maple
A low, spreading, mound-forming shrub with delicate foliage that colors well in the fall. 'Dissectum' has finely cut leaves.

Agave americana
Century plant
A bold rosette of strong, fleshy, pointed leaves, armed with sharp spikes along their margins. 'Marginata' has leaves edged with gold bands.

Astelia chathamica
Silver spear
Upright rosettes of silver-gray, sharply pointed foliage, reaching up to 5 ft (1.5 m) in length.

Brugmansia x candida 'Knightii'
Angels' trumpets
Tender plant with large, drooping, double flowers, creamy white and heavily scented. All parts are highly toxic if eaten.

Canna
Indian shot plant
Large, oval leaves, often bronze and sometimes finely striped in an array of red, orange, and cream shades. Showy, exotic-looking blooms are carried on tall stems; 'Assaut' has scarlet flowers; 'King Midas' has golden yellow flowers.

Dicksonia antarctica
Woolly tree fern
Very showy, unusual, treelike fern with a stout, fibrous trunk topped with wide-spreading, mid-green fronds. New fronds unfurl from tightly curled "croziers" in the center of the plant.

Fatsia japonica
Japanese aralia
Large, bold, palmshaped leaves of a deep, glossy green. Drumstick heads of small white flowers appear in the fall, turning to black fruits.

Laurus nobilis
Bay laurel
Pointed, dark green, aromatic leaves with small, fluffy yellow flowers in early spring. 'Aurea' has golden yellow foliage. Can be clipped to shape and trained as a standard. Contact with foliage may irritate skin.

Stipa gigantea
Giant feather grass
Arching mounds of slender, mid-green foliage and airy, feathery plumes of flowers carried on tall stems in late summer.

Trachycarpus fortunei
Chusan palm
Rounded, deeply divided, palmlike fronds are carried at the ends of long stems on top of a rough, fibrous trunk. Slow growing.

Yucca filamentosa
Adam's needle
Evergreen rosettes of long, swordshaped leaves with fibrous threads unraveling along their margins. Established plants bear panicles of creamy white, cupshaped flowers in summer. 'Variegata' has white-margined leaves, tinged pink in winter.

4

GIANT FEATHER GRASS

UNUSUAL FEATURES

Containers can be used to create an unusual and individual garden feature. An old bathtub or wheelbarrow makes an ideal showcase for a collection of special plants, while a teapot that has lost its handle or a favorite old pair of garden boots make whimsical outer pots.

MAKING A SCENE

■ **Full to the brim** A tall, elegant water jug filled with trailing plants such as deep blue anagallis and white-flowered sutera gives the effect of foaming water flowing out. Tilt the jug slightly to give the impression of contents spilling out.

■ **Alpine fresh** An old trough filled with alpine plants can nestle among scree and rocky outcrops to echo a mountainside scene.

■ **Secret dell** A hollowed-out log makes an excellent setting for ferns, violets, and other woodland plants.

■ **Along the coast** Rope-coiled pots or a disused lobster pot planted with sea holly, dorotheanthus, rosemary, and tamarisk can be set on pebbles, shells, and driftwood to conjure up a harborside setting.

■ **Forgotten corner** A tall, slender traditional-style chimney pot can be planted and wreathed with ivy to give a deliberate tumble-down effect.

STACKED TOGETHER
A selection of slender chimney pots filled with summer flowers adds old-world charm to the tumble-down look of a cottage garden.

4

Window Boxes

5

WINDOW BOXES

Lushly planted window boxes really help to strengthen the link between a house and its garden, by echoing the style and colors of a planting theme. In courtyard gardens and on apartment balconies they provide virtually all of the growing space available. They not only improve and enhance the appearance of the building from the outside, but when planted with a well thought-out scheme, they can be appreciated just as much from within the home as without.

There are many practical points to bear in mind when fixing and planting window boxes, to make sure that they are safe, easy to care for, and have long-lasting appeal. Herbs and foliage plants can be used as well as flowers, and scented plants are particularly welcome beneath an open window, where their scent can drift into the house.

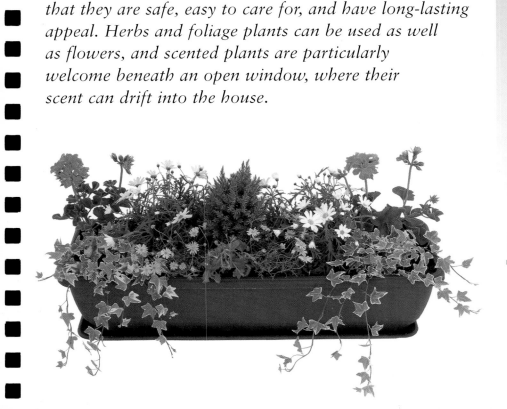

5

WINDOW DRESSING

Designed to suit platforms and ledges, window boxes are low, rectangular troughs, which can be fixed to external walls, just below the level of a window. They make use of otherwise sterile wall space, and are particularly important for houses without gardens where, along with hanging baskets, they provide a vital growing area.

POINTS TO CONSIDER

■ **Light-saving** Exactly where a window box should be positioned depends to some extent on the style of the window. It may seem obvious to stand the window box on an outer sill, but this is not always practical. Unless the windows are tall, the box and the plants it contains are going to block out quite a lot of light from the room. If casement-type windows that open outward have been fitted, a box will prevent them from being opened. For this reason, sash or inward-opening windows are better suited to having window boxes placed in front of them.

■ **Secure fixing** It is essential that window boxes are fixed securely. This protects your plants and passersby from damage and injury should the box become dislodged in bad weather or accidentally knocked off. In general, it is best to attach boxes below the sill (see pp. 84–85).

■ **Room with a view** Window boxes make the outside of the building more attractive, but they can also be appreciated from the inside, too – a fact that is sometimes forgotten when planning their planting. Rather than creating a one-sided display that is best enjoyed by your neighbors, arrange the plants in an evenly balanced display so that you can appreciate them from indoors, too.

■ **Alternative uses** Window boxes do not always have to be positioned outside windows. They can be used as freestanding troughs on walls or steps; they also look effective when secured to railings, particularly on balconies, or used to decorate the roof of a garden shed. A dull, blank wall can be easily livened up by painting on some representations of simple window frames and fixing window boxes below them to form an effective *trompe l'oeil*.

5

LIGHTWEIGHT PLASTIC WINDOW BOX

Drip tray stops water from spilling over

ROOM WITH A VIEW
Scarlet-red pelargoniums make
an eye-catching contribution
to this floral window display.

SIZE AND SHAPE

Most window boxes are rectangular, but their
size varies considerably. If the box is to be fixed
below the window sill, you will not be restricted
to finding one that fits the space exactly; for the
most pleasing effect, try to keep the length of
the box in proportion to the width and the height
of the window. The best appearance is usually
obtained from a window box that is slightly
wider than the window, and you may find that you
need to use two boxes to fill the space available.
Remember that a deep box retains moisture better,
but if a deep box is placed on a window sill it
will block too much light from the room.

Warning

Bear in mind that
deep window boxes
are very heavy once
they have been filled
with soil and plants.
Take care when lifting
and moving them, and
check that they are
fixed securely in place.

5

FLOWERING LEDGES

When choosing a window box it is particularly important to select one that will blend happily with the style of your house, as the window box will become a fixture of the house itself. However eye-catching the plants, an inappropriate box will jar and spoil the display.

THE RIGHT TYPE

Most window boxes are made from wood, plastic, fiberglass, or terra-cotta. Given that window boxes are invariably suspended off the ground, it is best to keep the weight of the box to a minimum so as to reduce stress on the fixings. A lightweight box will also be easier to handle if you need to move the box to a more convenient place when tending to your plants. Alternatively, choose a plain, lightweight trough as the inner container, which can then be housed in a more decorative outer box.

Window boxes usually follow the same formal pattern in which house windows are arranged; where more than two or more boxes are used, make sure that they are all the same style to create a coherent effect. Wooden boxes can be painted to blend with the house, or to give them a distinctive individual style.

HUES OF BLUE
A cool-colored planting scheme of low-growing and trailing blue-flowered plants provides a refreshing window-box display.

5

TOP TIPS

• A spare inner container can be prepared with fresh plants as an instant replacement for a fading display.

• Painted walls and white-curtained windows make good backdrops for bold, colorful plantings.

• Apply a plant-safe, weatherproof preservative to wooden troughs before planting up (see p. 15).

PURE PINK
A single-color scheme of trailing pelargoniums, valued for their drought-resistance, provides summer-long interest.

WATERING AND DRAINAGE

Like all containers, window boxes hold a relatively small amount of soil, which gives rise to the usual problems of regulating the water supply. Because window boxes are sheltered from rainfall by their position against the house, they will need frequent watering. This can be a problem if access to them is difficult. If a window box is fixed below the level of an upper-story window sill, it should be possible to water the plants by reaching through the window. If the window opens outward, however, the plants may eventually grow too tall for the window to be opened without damaging them. If it is not possible to water plants through the adjacent window, you may need to use an attachment to your watering system to help you reach. Various hose fittings and devices are available to make watering from below easier (see p. 99).

Water must also be able to drain away from a box – but preferably not down the wall of the house, where it can leave unattractive stains and possibly cause damp to penetrate the wall. Like any other container, a window box should have drainage holes in its base, preferably situated toward the front of the box, keeping the drainage water clear of the wall. A drip tray fitted below a window box is useful to prevent water from overspilling, but do not allow the box to remain standing in water.

5

PLANTING UP

Before starting to plant a window box or trough, you need to decide whether it will be practical to transport and fix the container in position after planting, or whether it will be best to part plant or postpone planting until it has been placed in its final position. Once the box has been filled with soil, planted up, and watered, it is too late to discover that it is heavy and awkward to maneuver through the window frame or to carry up a ladder. If planting up the box *in situ* is likely to be difficult, then look for a lightweight container that will fit comfortably inside your window box. This "inner box" can then be planted up and placed into the fixed "outer" window box.

STEP-BY-STEP PLANTING

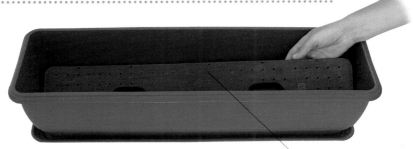

Internal reservoir ensures constant water supply

1 When planting directly into the window box, check that there are sufficient drainage holes in the base. Make additional holes, if necessary, and cover these with crocks and a layer of coarse gravel to ensure they do not become blocked. An internal reservoir tray may be fitted in the base of the window box to ensure a constant supply of water for the plants.

5

Water-retaining granules absorb and release moisture

2 Half-fill the box with a lightweight, potting soilless mix; supplement the mix with water-retaining granules and slow-release fertilizer, applied at the manufacturer's recommended rate.

Trailing plants will
curtain trough front

Young evergreen adds
height to display

3 Position the plants (still in their
pots) in the window box to achieve
the best arrangement of their upright,
flowering, or trailing features. If your
box is to be visible from both sides,
adjust the planting to ensure a well-
balanced, all-round display.

4 Once the plants are arranged to
your satisfaction, ease each plant
gently out of its pot and insert firmly
in the soil. Seasonal plants can be set
within separate pots to make them
easier to remove once they have passed
their best and are ready to be replaced.

5

5 Position any individually potted
plants within the window box,
and fill in around and over the top of
them with soil mix so that they are
completely concealed. Water the
arrangement well, then fix the
window box securely into position.

6 As individual plants start to fade,
the inner containers in which they
are growing can be removed without
disturbing the long-term plants.
Replace them with an appropriate
seasonal plant that is ready to flower,
water well and enjoy the display.

FIXING A WINDOW BOX

E ven on the ground floor, a window box that falls from its position
means a ruined display, wasting your time and money. Secure
fixing is therefore very important, and as far as safety is concerned,
its importance increases the higher up the window box is displayed.

USING THE WINDOW SILL

A planted-up window box is
surprisingly heavy. Its long, narrow
shape – and often narrow base – can
also make it unstable, especially as
the plants grow in size. If a window
box is positioned on an upper-story
window sill it must be sitting on a
level surface and properly secured
with hooks and screws to prevent it
from falling or being knocked off.
To avoid a potentially lethal accident,
run through the following checklist:

■ **Window opening** Check which
way a window opens before siting
a window box in front of it. If the

window opens outward, it be will
obstructed by the box and you will
not be able to use it for ventilation.

■ **Sound window sill** The sill must
be broad and sturdy enough to hold
the weight of a freshly watered box
at the peak of its growth.

■ **Sloping sills** Most window sills
slope downward in order to drain
water away from the window frame,
so wedges need to be placed under
the front edge of the window box
to level it. This will also improve
drainage from the base of the box.

KIT FOR FIXING A WINDOW BOX
BENEATH A CASEMENT WINDOW

Fixings

Adjustment to fit
brackets to
width of box

Wall bracket

Window-box
support

5

SAFETY

If you decide to use
an electric drill or any
electric power tool
outdoors, make sure
that is is fitted with
a circuit breaker. This
device will cut the
power supply almost
instantly if a fault is
detected in the circuit.
Always disconnect the
power if you need to
inspect the drill or
to change a bit and
keep spare cable to
a minimum so that
you do not trip over
or damage it.

FIXING TIPS

If you are positioning your window box below the sill, it must be securely attached to the wall with L-shaped or angle brackets. First, screw the brackets to each side of the box, and then to the wall.

■ **Fixings** When fixing brackets to walls, drill holes with a masonry bit and use a special wall plug fixing which will ensure that the bracket is held securely in the brickwork. Alternatively, use wooden dowels inserted into holes drilled in the brickwork, fixing the screws for the brackets into the ends of the dowels.

■ **Making a ledge** To make a ledge for the window box to sit on, screw two or more (depending on the length of the box) sturdy metal brackets directly into the wall at a suitable distance below the window sill; a piece of timber can be fixed across the brackets to make a solid shelf, if desired.

BRIGHTER BRICKWORK

• When hanging troughs to relieve the monotony of a plain brick wall, position them at different heights to divert the eye away from the parallel rows of bricks.

• Avoid positioning window boxes one directly beneath the other as the lower box will be set in shade and receive less rainfall.

• Create a tiered focal point in your garden by placing a ground-level grouping of containers below an arrangement of window boxes on a wall. Repeat a key color, container style, or range of plants throughout the display for maximum impact.

• Create a showcase on which to display your boxes. Fix a series of shelves on the wall and encase them with a frame. Alternate two different styles or colors of boxes along the shelves for a striking effect.

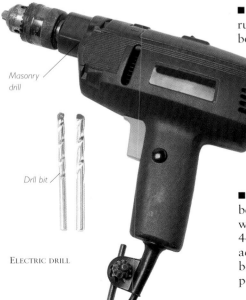

Masonry drill

Drll bit

ELECTRIC DRILL

■ **Adding chains** For extra security, run chains from the front edge of the box to the window frame, hooking them into metal eyes at each end.

■ **Using wall mangers** Wrought-iron mangers may be fixed to the walls below windows. These look attractive even when empty, and can be used to hold a lightweight window box.

■ **Metal bar** A slim metal bar can be fixed as a restraint across the width of the window frame, about 4–6 in (10–15 cm) above the sill. This acts as a reassuring check that the box cannot fall, and allows small pots to be stood on the sill, too.

5

WINTER WINDOW BOX

Generally, window boxes tend to be regarded as summer fixtures – emptied as soon as the first frost arrives, and stored away until the following spring. They can, however, provide plenty of interest during other seasons, even in the depths of winter.

STRIKING WHITES

Although *Helleborus niger* is commonly known as the Christmas rose, the wide, saucerlike blooms do not usually appear until early January in the open garden. In a sheltered window box, Christmas roses will bloom earlier; their sheltered position and the warmth radiated through the house walls, means that the plants are less subject to weather damage.

Borne on sturdy purple-marked stems, the ivory-white flowers boast a central boss of gold stamens. They will remain perfect in their elevated position, and can be appreciated more easily than when they are nodding at ground level.

For a dramatic contrast in your planting, add *Helleborus* x *hybridus* 'Ballard's Black', which bears deep, dark purple flowers or *H.* x *h.* 'Peggy Ballard', with its large flowers colored dark red on the outside and heavily veined dusky-pink inside.

Common snowdrops *(Galanthus nivalis)* make the perfect partners in a winter window box; the single varieties, such as *G. n.* 'Scharlockii' and *G. n.* 'Sandersii', have more elegance and grace than the stocky, frilly edged doubles. Their dainty, nodding white flowers often bear green markings or, in the case of 'Scharlockii', pale yellow markings and a yellow base.

Curling tendrils of a white-variegated ivy such as *Hedera helix* 'Glacier' complete the snowy theme. They can be trailed down the sides of the window box to soften the hard edges of the container.

5

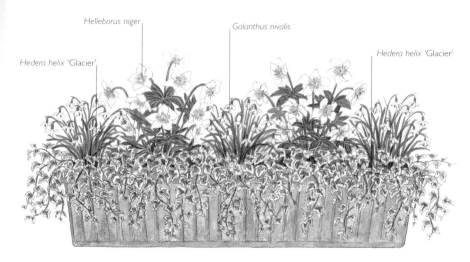

Helleborus niger

Galanthus nivalis

Hedera helix 'Glacier'

Hedera helix 'Glacier'

SPRING PLEASURES

Flowering spring bulbs are always among the most welcome plants in the garden and need little in the way of elaborate styling to give a cheerful display. A bold and simple contrast of colors, interspersed with bright green foliage, makes a most effective window box.

FRESH BLOOMS

The hardy grape hyacinth (*Muscari armeniacum*) is a prolific plant; its bellshaped flowers, which are clustered on short stems like bunches of grapes, are an intense, bright blue, an unusual shade among spring bulbs. *M. a.* 'Early Giant' has large, deep cobalt-blue blooms that have a pleasant perfume.

The buttercup-yellow flowers of the dwarf daffodil *Narcissus* 'Tête-à-Tête' contrast well with grape hyacinths. Its slightly nodding flowers are perfect golden trumpet daffodils in miniature.

For the best flowering display, raise the bulbs in pots until the flowerbuds have formed, then transfer them to the window box to flower; this gives more control over the final result than planting directly into the box.

SPRING BULBS

Below is a small selection of the many small, spring-flowering bulbs suitable for growing in containers.

• *Anemone blanda* 'Ingramii'

• *Crocus chrysanthus* 'Eye-catcher'; *C. c.* 'Snow Bunting'; *C. minimus*

• *Hyacinthus orientalis* 'Ostara'; *H. o.* 'Delft Blue'; *H. o.* 'City of Haarlem'

• *Iris danfordiae*; *Iris winogradowii*

• Dwarf tulips *(Tulipa)*: Choose from the Kaufmanniana and Greigii groups

• Dwarf daffodils *(Narcissus)*: Choose from the Triandrus, Cyclamineus, and Jonquilla groups

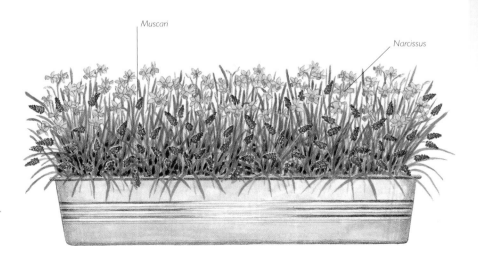

Muscari

Narcissus

5

SUMMER SPECIALS

The vast array of colors offered by summer flowers often tempts us to throw caution aside and go for a "riot of color" approach when planting. This does not always work successfully within the confined space of a window box, making individual colors look "spotty" and disjointed. A restrained color scheme is usually more satisfying.

SUNNY SPLENDOR

Yellow is always a popular color, with its sunny, cheerful effect. There are many shades of yellow, from gentlest pastel primrose to glowing golden orange; all can be offset attractively by fresh green foliage.

Creeping zinnia *(Sanvitalia procumbens)* and its cultivars make a popular container plant, valued for their long flowering period from early summer to early fall. Large numbers of bright yellow daisylike flowers with distinctive black eyes spangle the foliage in summer. S. p. 'Gold Braid' is a compact variety; the dwarf creeping zinnia S. p. 'Golden Carpet' produces small, lemon flowers that are set off against very dark green foliage.

The large many-petaled flowers of *Gazania* Daybreak Series closely resemble small sunflowers. The flower centers are accentuated by a brown ring, and petal colors range from creamy yellow through gold and orange to deep mahogany, some with contrasting stripes. All of the shades blend well together and are enhanced by the deep green, linear leaves with silver, felted undersides.

Another plant with soft-haired foliage is helichrysum *(Helichrysum petiolare)* whose woolly, semi-trailing stems are set with neat, oval leaves covered in fine hairs. *H. p.* 'Limelight' has lime-green foliage; *H. p.* 'Variegatum' has gray leaves, with cream variegation.

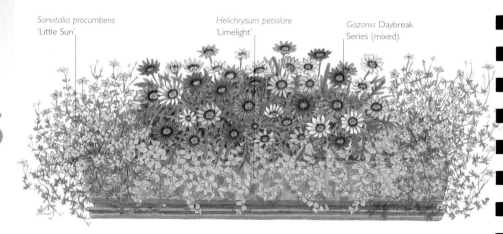

Sanvitalia procumbens 'Little Sun'

Helichrysum petiolare 'Limelight'

Gazania Daybreak Series (mixed)

5

Artemisia schmidtiana 'Nana'

Osteospermum 'Silver Sparkler'

Felicia amelloides 'Read's Blue'

Anagallis monelli 'Skylover'

Helichrysum petiolare

COLOR CHOICES

YELLOW	BLUE
Chrysanthemum multicaule 'Moonlight'	**Ageratum 'Blue Mist'**
Dorotheanthus bellidiformis 'Lunette'	**Brachyscome 'Blue Mist'** Swan river daisy
Lotus maculatus	**Convolvulus sabatius** Bindweed
Lamium maculatum 'Cannon's Gold' Dead nettle	**Lobelia erinus 'Crystal Palace'; L. e. 'Sapphire'**
Nemesia strumosa Triumph Series	**Nemesia strumosa 'Blue Gem'**
Thymophylla tenuiloba Golden fleece	**Plumbago auriculata** Cape leadwort
Viola Crystal Bowl Series (yellow) Pansy	**Scaevola aemula** Fairy fan-flower
	Surfinia 'Violet Blue'

COOL BLUES

At the opposite end of the color spectrum, blue shades offer a cool and sophisticated effect and look particularly good against a white background. *Artemisia schmidtiana* 'Nana', a perennial wormwood, has very finely cut, silver-blue foliage that makes a series of overlapping rosettes to form a distinctive rounded mound. The vigorous blue daisy, *Felicia amelloides* 'Read's Blue' has strong blue petals offset by yellow centers. The informal outline and saucer-shaped flowers of blue pimpernel, here *Anagallis monelli* 'Skylover', tumble over the front of the box.

The inclusion of white flowers in a scheme usually helps to highlight blue shades more effectively. This planting is lightened by the cream-variegated foliage of *Osteospermum* 'Silver Sparkler', with sparkling white flowers pierced by powder-blue centers. The cool tone is continued with the silver, furry stems of *Helichrysum petiolare*.

5

WINDOWBOX HERBS

Culinary herbs have so many qualities – they look attractive, smell wonderful, and turn almost any food you prepare into something special. A window box is, in many ways, an ideal place in which to grow herbs, keeping them close at hand so they are ready to use.

COOK'S DELIGHT

Most compact herbs suit window boxes, although large, shrubby kinds raised as rooted cuttings or small plants will tolerate the confines of a box for up to three years.

■ **Preparation** Clean and prepare the window box, ensuring adequate drainage and using a good quality potting soil mix (see pp. 82–83). Most gardening experts advise against giving herbs too much fertilizer, as strong, lush growth is less aromatic than the hard growth produced by poor soil. Apply a moderate amount of slow-release fertilizer to encourage plenty of new

growth to replace shoot tips as they are harvested. Most herbs are perennial, but if you cut window box herbs regularly, you may find it more useful to treat them as annuals.

■ **Siting** Ideally, herbs should be placed where they will receive at least some direct sun daily. Place the box by a window that can be opened, so that you can pick the herbs and enjoy their aroma.

HERBS GALORE
With its good looks and tasty foliage, a tiered trough crammed full of kitchen herbs will delight cooks and gardeners alike.

5

HERBS FOR CONTAINERS

Ocimum spp.
Basil
• Greek or bush basil
(O. campechianum var.
minimum) is ideal for
growing in small
containers. Its clove-
scented leaves are good
with tomato dishes. O.
basilicum 'Spicy Globe'
makes a compact plant.
• Can be harvested until
late fall.
• Raise from seed.

Anthriscus cerefolium
Chervil
• Soft, lacy, fernlike leaves
have a mild aniseed flavor.
• Useful in salads and
with eggs.
• Raise from seed.

Allium schoenopraseum
Chives
• Grassy upright leaves
are onionflavored.
• Harvest by cutting the
leaves right to the base
with sharp scissors.
• Buy young plants.

MINT

Origanum
Marjoram
• Sweet marjoram
(Origanum majorana) has
a warm, sweet fragrance.
• Good with chicken
dishes and tomatoes.
• Buy young plants.

Mentha
Mint
• Mint is a rampant
grower so confine it to
an individual pot sunk
in the soil.
• Pineapple mint (M.
suaveolens 'Variegata') has
creamy variegated leaves;
ginger mint (M. x gracilis)
is beautifully veined gold.
• Buy young plants.

Petroselinum
Parsley
• Curled, frilly leaved
parsley(such as P. crispum
'Afro') has mossy, deep
green foliage that suits
decorative use.
• Flat-leaved varieties,
such as French or Italian
parsley (P. crispum var.
neapolitanum), have the
best flavor.
• Grow as an annual
from seed. Presoak the
seed in hot water to
speed up germination.

Rosmarinus
Rosemary
• Pretty blue flowers and
silvery, needlelike leaves
with a distinctive aroma.
• Use the low-growing,
creeping rosemary
(R. Prostratus Group)
for window boxes.
• Good for flavoring oils
and vinegars.
• Buy young plants.

SAGE

Salvia
Sage
• Gray-green, wrinkled
leaves have a warm and
pungent scent.
• Salvia 'Icterina' has
creamy yellow foliage.
• Buy young plants.
• The leaves of scarlet
or red sage (S. coccinea)
can be dried for use in
potpourri.

Artemisia dracunculus
Tarragon
• Slender, spearshaped
leaves have a minty
aniseed flavor.
• Buy young plants; seed-
raised tarragon is said to
have an inferior flavor.

Thymus spp.
Thyme
• Thyme's tiny, oval leaves
are intensely fragrant.
• Ideal for growing in
window boxes.
• Lemon thyme
(T. x citriodorus) is
a culinary favorite.
• Buy young plants.

5

THE VALUE OF FOLIAGE

By far the majority of window boxes are filled with flowering plants, but a foliage-only box can make a refreshing change. The subtle blend of cool green shades creates a lush effect for hot, parched summer days and contrasts with other boxes brimming with flowers.

FOLIAGE FAVORITES

■ **Senecio** *Senecio cineraria* 'Silver Dust' has bright silver, lacy, deeply cut leaves while *S. c.* 'Cirrus' has round, silver-white leaves with less deeply indented margins.

■ **Coleus or painted nettle** *Solenostemon scutellarioides* has serrated-edged foliage in a stunning assortment of brilliant colors. *S. c.* 'Pineapple Beauty' has yellow-green leaves with purple markings *S. c.* 'Royal Scot' has bright red leaves with khaki centers.

■ **Perilla** *Perilla frutescens* var. *crispa* has deep bronze-purple foliage with serrated, crisped, and wavy margins.

■ **Burning bush** The soft, light green leaves of the coniferlike *Bassia scoparia f. trichophylla* turn bright red or purple toward fall.

■ **Houseleeks** *Sempervivum* are evergreen succulents with rosettes of thick, pointed leaves. The cobweb houseleek *(S. arachnoideum)* is coated in soft white hairs; the vigorous-growing common houseleek *(S. tectorum)* has blue-green to red-purple leaves.

FLATTERING FOLIAGE
The broad, lush-green leaves of the hosta and delicately variegated ivy uplift this small group of containers in a shady corner.

5

COMPACT SHRUBS

Although shrubs and subshrubs may eventually outgrow a window box, some make worthwhile short-term tenants. Spotted laurel *(Aucuba japonica)* is an excellent choice for a winter box; particularly variegated varieties, such as the yellow-speckled 'Gold Dust'. Several hebes are also suitable, including *Hebe × andersonii* 'Variegata', which is freely available as a small plant. Spindle tree *(Euonymus)* is another good choice, particularly variegated varieties such as *Euonymus fortunei* 'Harlequin' and *E. f.* 'Emerald 'n' Gold'.

Dwarf conifers provide variations in color, form, and texture in a window box, from the upright, deep green column of the common juniper *(Juniperus communis* 'Compressa') to the starry blue pyramid of the spruce, *Picea glauca* 'Alberta Blue', and the fluffy textured, bronze-green Japanese cedar *Cryptomeria japonica* 'Vilmoriniana'.

CREEPERS AND TRAILERS

Many foliage plants are widely used as trailing subjects in mixed plantings. *Glechoma hederacea*, *Helichrysum petiolare*, and *Lamium maculatum* are among the most popular, and an exciting range of colored and variegated forms is available.

Coral gem *(Lotus berthelotii)* has, in warm summers, showy scarlet blooms, but it is valued for its cascades of silver, needlelike foliage. The variety names of creeping bugle *(Ajuga reptans)* – 'Burgundy Glow', 'Multicolor', 'Pink Splendor', 'Purple Brocade', and 'Silver Shadow' – give an idea of the wide range of color forms that exist.

Attractive variegated leaf adds color interest

VARIEGATED TRAILING IVY

5

FINE FRAGRANCE

Scented plants are the perfect choice for planting in window boxes with the window open, their fragrance can drift into the house on the warm summer air. Scent from flowers is the most valuable, as it is freely released; fragrance from aromatic foliage can usually only be appreciated if the leaves have been bruised or handled.

CHOOSING SCENTS

Flowers generally have sweet scents, which in most cases, it is impossible to describe accurately, although "honeylike," "fruity," or "spicy" may give an idea of their fragrance. The appreciation of fragrance is a very personal sensation, and what is a strong, pleasant scent to one person can appear light or even nonexistent to someone else.

Sadly, some modern varieties of plants that were once well known for their scent may no longer have any fragrance – the perfume has been bred out of them in the quest for other attributes. This may apply particularly to plants that are suitable for window boxes, as modern, dwarf varieties often seem to have sacrificed scent for compact growth. Dwarf varieties of pinks *(Dianthus)*, sweet peas *(Lathyrus)*, and flowering tobacco *(Nicotiana)* all need to be selected carefully to ensure the ones chosen retain a reasonable perfume.

Many flowers release most of their perfume in the early evening, and this is often the best time to enjoy a scented window box. Fragrance may also be intensified by a shower of rain – an effect that can be re-created by watering a plant lightly with a fine spray fitted on a watering can.

Plants with aromatic foliage often have insignificant flowers, but this is a small price to pay for their sensual delights. Scented-leaved pelargoniums, for example, make a valuable addition to a box, offering a range of aromas from apple, lemon, and orange to nutmeg and balsam. As is the case with all aromatic foliage, be sure to plant them within reach where they can be gently squeezed in passing to release their heady scents.

LAVENDER SPRIG

5

SCENTED FLOWERS

Dianthus (dwarf varieties)
Pinks

Exacum affine
Persian violet

Heliotropum peruvianum
Cherry pie

Hyacinthus orientalis
Hyacinth

Laurentia axillaris
Shooting stars

Lathyrus odorata (dwarf varieties)
Sweet pea

Lavandula species
Lavender

Nemesia denticulata

Nicotiana hybrids
Flowering tobacco

Verbena hybrids

NICOTIANA 'LIME GREEN'

Hanging baskets
and wall pots

6

HANGING BASKETS AND WALL POTS

Hanging baskets add a completely new dimension to a garden. Like window boxes and wall pots, they do not require any ground space at all, so they can be used very successfully to decorate homes that have no gardens. Their care can sometimes be difficult, but using a few simple tricks when planting and hanging will help to ensure a trouble-free, long-lasting display.

Although baskets and wall pots are usually features of summer gardens, there is no reason why they cannot be decorative through the winter months and into spring as well. They can even be used to grow food crops, providing a miniature kitchen garden.

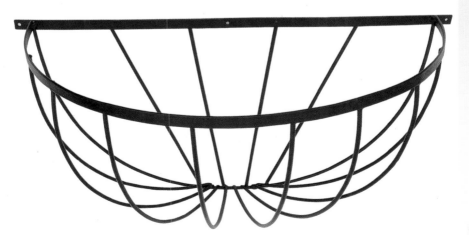

6

HANGING BASKETS

Unlike other types of plant containers, hanging baskets are designed to be viewed mainly from below. With a little skill and careful planning, you can create a stunning sphere of color, such that the container itself is completely hidden by flowers and foliage.

BASKET STYLES

■ **Open sided** The traditional basket is made from plastic-coated wire, and can be hemispherical, hexagonal, or bowl shaped with a flattened base. When choosing a wire basket, make sure the spaces between the wires are large enough to insert plants through, otherwise the point of such a basket is lost.

■ **Solid sided** The main advantage of hanging containers with solid sides is that they conserve water. Trailing plants can be set around the edges of the basket so that they hang down and disguise the container itself, but the effect is never quite as dramatic as a traditional wire basket with plants emerging through the side walls. Because the sides are more likely to be seen, look for containers made from materials that have an interesting texture or design; for example, coiled-rope, wicker, and stained wood versions all provide an attractive backdrop for plantings.

■ **Basket pillar** If you do not have any available hanging space in your garden, but would still like to have a basket feature, choose a freestanding basket pillar (see p. 12). Basket pillars comprise three or four tiers of wire, hemispherical baskets, fixed to a central stem. The baskets are arranged by size, with the smallest at the top of the pillar. When fully planted, they create an attractive cascade of flowers and foliage.

HEXAGONAL
WIRE BASKET

Trailing foliage can
be trained around
wire framework

■ **Flower tower** This comprises a shallow bowl and hanging frame joined together by a long tube of polyethylene. The tube is filled with soil mix, and the walls are pierced with planting holes. Plants soon cover the entire tower, and the bowl at the base acts as a water reservoir, making routine care easy.

6

BASKET LININGS

The one major drawback of hanging baskets is that they dry out extremely quickly. To hold the soil mix in place and to keep moisture loss to a minimum, all open-sided baskets need to be lined. Remember that open, porous lining materials such as moss and grass clippings need to be partly covered with a sheet of pierced polyethylene before soil mix and plants are added to the basket, otherwise water drains through them too rapidly.

■ **Moss** Sphagnum moss still has much to commend for lining baskets. It looks attractive, holds moisture well, and allows plants to be inserted around the sides of the basket. Compressed, dried moss (harvested from renewable resources) is available as shaped liners or in small bales, swelling to shape rapidly once watered; it is easy and convenient to buy and to use.

■ **Grass** Clippings of grass collected by the lawn mower can be recycled for basket lining, though they need to be wilted by just the right amount to make them manageable – leave them in a heap for a day or two before use.

■ **Liners** Proprietary liners are made from substances such as coir fiber, wool and wood waste, pulped paper, or plastic, and usually cut or molded to fit a specific size of basket. They are all effective at holding in soil and moisture but some are difficult to pierce with holes or do not allow any side planting – which defeats the object of using a traditional-style open-weave wire basket.

MOLDED, RIGID LINER

COMPRESSED MOSS LINER

Shaped to fit circular baskets

COIR-FIBER LINER

SPHAGNUM MOSS

6

HANGING THE BASKETS

The ideal position for hanging baskets is at a suitable height to prevent them from getting in the way, but not so far out of reach that watering becomes impossibly difficult. The basket will need several hours of sunshine but some light shade for part of each day to cut down water loss; it should also be sheltered from winds.

FIRMLY FIXED

Most hanging baskets are supported by three chains evenly spaced around the rim and brought together at a large hook above the top of the basket. While the basket is being planted up, the chains can be removed to prevent them from getting in the way, but make sure that the plants are not positioned where they will be damaged by the chains once they are linked up again for hanging.

   Although a hanging basket is quite small, it is, like most containers, surprisingly heavy when fully planted and watered; for this reason, a sturdy support system is essential. In some cases a basket can hang from a simple hook fixed to the overhead beam of a pergola or porch, for example, but usually a bracket is necessary to hold the basket away from a wall. The safest type is a triangular rather than an L-shaped bracket, with a diagonal strut to help spread the load. Some baskets are not suspended from the bracket but designed to fit on top of it instead, held in place by a upward-facing spike that fits in a socket. This

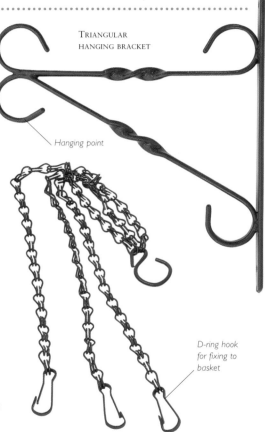

TRIANGULAR HANGING BRACKET

Hanging point

D-ring hook for fixing to basket

HANGING CHAINS AND HOOK

arrangement eliminates having to use chains, which can restrict the plants' growth. A padlock can also be fitted through the spike and socket to prevent baskets from being stolen.

6

WATERING

It is hardly any wonder that hanging baskets dry out so rapidly: they are shallow and densely planted, the soil is exposed to the air, and they are hung in open positions, where they are exposed to full sun and drying winds. The majority of baskets require watering at least daily during the summer, sometimes twice a day, and any steps that can be taken to make watering easier are worthwhile. Always allow space for watering when filling and planting up the basket (see pp. 100–101).

■ **Pulley systems** A simple pulley device will enable high baskets to be lowered to a more convenient height for watering and maintenance.

■ **Within reach** Hang the baskets where they can be watered easily.

■ **Water reservoir** If watering your basket on a daily basis is not convenient to your schedule, opt

FLOWERING BELLES
Whether planted up with a single- or mixed-color scheme, hanging baskets provide a most satisfying way to display summer flowers.

for self-watering hanging baskets. Fitted with built-in water reservoirs, these supply water to the soil via capillary-action matting.

■ **Watering can** Purposemade, pump-action watering cans are available for reaching high baskets, if a hose is not available.

■ **Flow control** When using a hose, adjust the flow to a gentle trickle; too much pressure will wash plants and soil out of the basket.

■ **Hose extension** A watering lance, with a long, rigid stem and down-turned tip can be fixed to the end of a hose to water above head height.

■ **Water-retaining granules** Added to the soil, these granules are useful in all types of container (see p. 45).

6

PLANTING BASKETS

It is worth taking the time and trouble to plant up a traditional hanging basket, to be rewarded with a spectacular feature for many weeks over the summer. Stand the planted basket in a sheltered place for several days before hanging so that the plants can begin to establish themselves. When you are hanging the basket, ask someone to take the weight of it from below.

TRADITIONAL STYLE

1 Support the empty basket firmly on a large pot or bucket for planting, temporarily removing the chains if they are likely to get in the way. Line the basket with your chosen material. Position a square of pierced plastic or a saucer on top of the lining at the base of the basket to prevent water draining through the liner too freely. Fill one-third of the basket with potting soil mix – a soil-based mix retains moisture better than soilless, but can make the completed basket too heavy. Add water-retaining granules and slow-release fertilizer, applied at the manufacturer's recommended rate.

Make slit central to basket hole

2 Using a sharp blade make 1-in (2.5-cm) slits through the liner at even spaces around the basket. These slits will allow you to insert small flowering plants and trailing foliage to ensure full coverage of the wire framework.

6

3 Insert the trailing plants through the sides of the basket. It is usually easiest to push the roots of the plants through from the outside, spreading them out on the soil; for other plants it may be easier to gently pull their topgrowth through from the inside of the basket. If plants are awkward to position, gently wash some of the soil off the roots and wrap the plant in a cone of newspaper to protect it as you insert it through the side of the basket.

Guide plant through from the outside

4 Top up with more soil mix, firming the plants in gently. Add another layer of plants through the side, if desired, until the basket is almost full. Plant the top of the basket with bushy and trailing plants, with an upright in the center to add height. Firm them in and water well.

6

WINTER BASKET

Of all plant containers, hanging baskets are the most difficult to keep going successfully through the winter months and virtually impossible in extreme climates. However, if you can find a sheltered sunny spot, out of the way of icy winds, perhaps close to the house, it is possible to create an attractive winter display.

VELVET TOUCH

Pansies *(Viola x wittrockiana)* are among the most reliable winter-flowering plants. Their main flushes of bloom are in fall and spring, but in sheltered positions they will carry on flowering through the winter. The Universal Series is perhaps the best-known variety, but several others offer a wide range of colors and petal markings too. Pansies can be planted both through the sides of baskets and around the top.

Ivy *(Hedera helix)* is hardy and tough and will help to cover the base of the basket with its trailing stems. A dark, glossy green shows off the colors of the pansies well, and a variety such as 'Green Ripple' has interestingly shaped foliage.

Winter-flowering heather provides some height in the center of the basket; *Erica carnea* 'Ann Sparkes' has the double bonus of rose-purple flowers and bronze-red foliage.

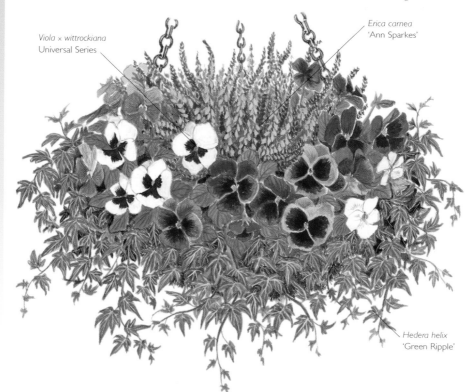

Viola x wittrockiana
Universal Series

Erica carnea
'Ann Sparkes'

Hedera helix
'Green Ripple'

6

WELCOMING SPRING

As the days lengthen, the choice of suitable flowering plants for a basket increases. Spring can be a treacherous time – hard frosts and chilling winds are just as likely as warm sunshine and soft breezes – so before hanging up the basket outdoors, remember to gradually harden off any plants that have been raised under glass.

RASPBERRY RIPPLE

Line the basket with moss, so that it will not matter that the basket sides can be seen as well as the plants. The most suitable trailing plant for a spring basket is, once again, ivy; this time a variegated variety such as green and white *Hedera helix* 'Glacier' brings a fresh, light note to this mainly pink and white scheme. Winter-flowering pansies have a renewed flush of bloom in spring; try one of the single-color varieties like this creamy white selection. The pompom flowers of double daisies *(Bellis perennis)* appear in early spring, in a variety of rosy pinks. *Anemone blanda* has deeply cut foliage and cheerful, daisy flowers that are freely produced; *A. b.* 'Radar' bears deep pink and white flowers. Both the daisies and anemones can be tucked at intervals through the sides of the basket, as well as being planted in the top.

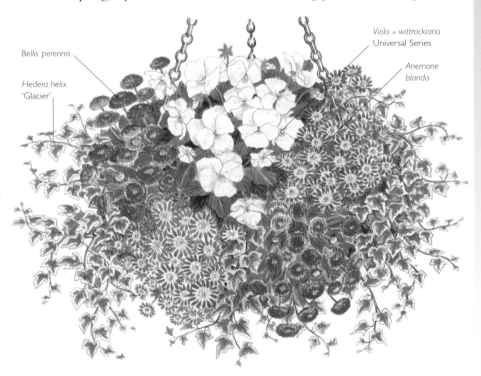

Bellis perennis

Hedera helix 'Glacier'

Viola × wittrockiana Universal Series

Anemone blanda

6

SUMMER SPLENDOR

The variety of plants suitable for summer hanging baskets is vast, and some wonderfully colorful, luxuriant displays can be created, with lush waterfalls of flowers and foliage. Before planting, consider whether you want a mass of color as a feature in its own right, or a themed color planting to be repeated in a number of baskets.

BLAZE OF COLOR

A mass of different colors works best in a basket displayed on its own, because it is difficult to reproduce a second basket, and two non-matching, boldly planted containers are likely to work against each other.

The 'Surfinia' varieties of petunias *(Petunia)* make strong, vigorous growth, even in poor weather conditions and produce numerous flowers, some with darker veining or a pronounced dark eye. The showy, cream-splashed leaves of the blue daisy, *Felicia amelloides* 'Santa Anita Variegated', provide foliage interest, and *Diascia* 'Coral Belle' has unusual lipped, salmon-pink flowers. A host of golden daisies on tumbling, bronze-foliaged stems is provided by *Sanvitalia* 'Little Sun', while the silver-leaved *Convolvulus sabatius* is set with clear blue, funnel-shaped blooms. The whole blaze of color is gently cooled down by the plain, silver foliage of the trailing *Helichrysum petiolare*.

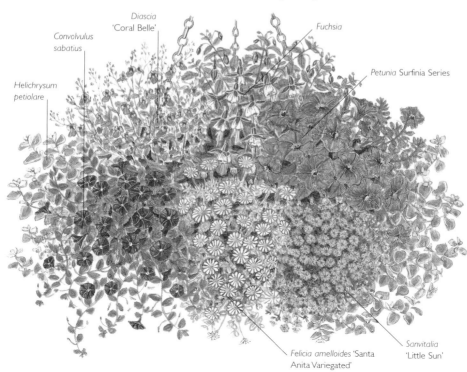

Diascia 'Coral Belle'

Convolvulus sabatius

Fuchsia

Helichrysum petiolare

Petunia Surfinia Series

Felicia amelloides 'Santa Anita Variegated'

Sanvitalia 'Little Sun'

IN THE PINK

A well-tended basket planted with a single plant variety can be every bit as eye-catching as a basket crammed with a whole range of different, multicolored plants. The type of plant chosen should be vigorous and free-flowering and you will need several plants for each basket. You will probably need to pinch and prune the stems carefully as they develop to obtain a good shape.

The specimen shown here is a trailing snapdragon, *Antirrhinum* 'Chandelier Rose Pink'. Its spreading, arching habit of growth makes it quite distinct from the common border snapdragons and is well suited for use in hanging baskets.

Other plants that suit a solo performance include nemesia, anagallis, trailing fuchsia, impatiens, ivy-leafed pelargonium, sutera, trailing petunia, and verbena. It is important that you make sure you buy plants of all the same variety for each basket – one of a different color would ruin the effect. Select plants in labeled pots, and reject any whose foliage color is markedly different to the others, as this often signifies a different flower color.

Fuchsias are excellent plants for hanging baskets and their drooping, bell-like flowers can be easily appreciated from below. Upright-growing varieties, such as *Fuchsia* 'Tom Thumb', are suitable for forming the center of a planting arrangement, while trailing types can cascade over the edges; there are also some semitrailing varieties of lax growth, which is somewhere between the two. *Fuchsia* 'Patio Princess' is a pretty bush variety with clear red sepals and double, frilled white petals.

Antirrhinum
'Chandelier Rose Pink'

Two-lipped
flower head

6

HARVEST FESTIVAL

No one can pretend that you will be able to keep yourself in homegrown vegetables from a few hanging baskets – but growing edible crops in baskets is great fun and always makes a good conversation piece. Hang vegetable baskets close to the kitchen for some really fresh garden produce.

COLORFUL SALADS

Salad vegetables are always welcome, even if there is only enough of a crop to make a garnish. Loose-leaf lettuce such as 'Salad Bowl' grows quite well in baskets, or try the mini-iceberg 'Blush', which grows 3–4 in (6–8 cm) across; trim away the spreading outer leaves as the heart develops. With their blue-green foliage and profusion of bold red, yellow, and orange flowers, nasturtiums *(Tropaeolum majus)* have an ideal trailing habit for baskets. Both the foliage and flowers are edible, adding a peppery taste and color to mixed salads.

KITCHEN HERBS

Herbs are well worth growing, as only small amounts need to be harvested for use. Many herbs are compact in habit and can tolerate relatively dry, poor conditions, so are well adapted to basket growing (see also p. 91).

• Basil *(Ocimum)*
• Parsley *(Petroselinum)*
• Rocket *(Eruca vesicaria)*
• Chives *(Allium schoenoprasum)*
• Summer savory *(Satureja)*
• Marjoram *(Origanum)*
• Oregano *(Origanum)*
• Rock hyssop *(Hyssopus)*
• Thyme *(Thymus)*
• Mint *(Mentha)*

TASTY VEGETABLES

Several vegetables are worth trying in baskets, too – and make an attractive display when interspersed with herbs.

■ **Tomato** The cherry-sized, bright red fruits of 'Tumbler', which has been specially bred for containers, are carried in abundance on trailing trusses and have an excellent flavor and handsome appearance. 'Phyra' is another cherry variety that grows well in baskets and other containers.

■ **Root vegetables** Carrots have very pleasing ferny foliage; try the variety 'Parmex', which produces small, globe-shaped roots with a sweet taste. Radishes are quick growing and tolerate crowded conditions. Choose a globe-rooted type such as 'Pink Beauty' or 'Scarlet Globe' for a hanging basket.

■ **Beans** Dwarf French beans make compact plants with clusters of slender pods that hang over the sides of the basket; grow and cook them with summer savory for a really special flavor.

■ **Peppers** Capsicum peppers vary in strength, from mild and sweet-tasting to very hot, but are striking to look at. 'Super Cayenne' grows well in containers and bears hot, deep red fruits; 'Firecracker' produces tiny, conical peppers of purple, orange, and red, and lives up to its name!

6

FRUIT DESSERTS

To round off a meal on the patio or just provide a sweet, summer snack, strawberries are perfect. Alpine varieties, with their tiny, intensely flavored fruits, are perhaps the best for hanging baskets; 'Mignonette' can be grown from seed and bears a particularly heavy crop. Large-fruited strawberries can also be grown, with

TRIUMPHANT ARCH
Glowing red tomatoes take pride of place in a display that is determined to catch the eye of visitors as they pass through the arch.

their clusters of fruit hanging attractively over the edge of the basket. Keep them well watered and fed, and pinch out runners as soon as they are formed to direct the plants' energy into fruit production.

6

GROUPING BASKETS

Perhaps more than most other types of containers, hanging baskets tend to be displayed in matching pairs, or in larger groups, and are rarely used for solo performances. Whether used in a formal or more casual arrangement, grouped baskets create a stunning effect.

FORMAL SITUATIONS

Hanging baskets are often used to add height, suspended from pillars or columns that form the framework of the garden. Filled with bold, simple arrangements, their purpose is to provide another tier to the planting scheme and to define the garden borders. Possibly the most popular position for baskets, though, is as a pair, flanking either side of a front door or gateway. For this formal arrangement to work well, the baskets and supporting brackets need to be as near identical as possible to achieve strong symmetry. Individual plantings will always differ slightly even if you have made every effort to use the same linings and varieties – two sets of plants simply will not grow and develop in exactly the same way. However, by using the same color scheme and balance of trailing, bushy, upright plants, a satisfactory result can be obtained. Sometimes the effect is spoiled because one basket develops more slowly than the other; this usually arises when one side of the grouping is in constant shade, or subject to cold winds. In this case, swap the positions of the baskets regularly to produce a more evenly balanced development.

FORMAL AND INFORMAL STYLE TIPS

FORMAL

• Highlight the geometry of the design, by repeating symmetrical plantings that use neat, strong shapes.

• Hang groups of baskets at an even height to maintain strong lines.

• Keep baskets in proportion to the design by using just one size of basket.

• Site hanging baskets to draw the eye to a focal point or vista, for example under an arch or either side of a gate.

• Train foliage-only baskets to create striking green globes, spirals, and mini-standards that mimic the geometrical shapes used in formal topiary.

INFORMAL

• Make the most of trailing plants and nodding flowers to produce organic, freeform shapes that soften harsh lines. Use trailing blue-flowered plants to mimic cascading water.

• Adapt unusual items, such as an old teapot, for use as containers (see p. 76) to achieve an unsophisticated look.

• Hang baskets at different heights to add interest to an arrangement. Grade the sizes of the baskets, with the smallest at the bottom and the largest at the top (or vice versa).

• Choose gentle, pastel shades to give a soft-focus effect to the planting scheme.

6

INFORMAL EFFECTS

In an informal arrangement, planting schemes can differ from basket to basket, although it does help the display if there is at least one common theme running through each of the baskets – the same variety of ivy, perhaps, or a white flowering plant occupying a prominent position in each.

An effective way to display two nonmatching baskets is to hang them slightly offset, one below the other,

and to use plant colors that make it look as though the plants are flowing from one basket to the next. For example, let a trailing white petunia spill over like white froth into a lower basket planted with matching white plants.

DECORATED BOUGHS
A well-established mature tree with bare lower boughs is given a new lease on life by a pair of colorful baskets hung from its branches.

6

WALL CONTAINERS

Like hanging baskets, wall pots and mangers offer an ideal solution for breaking up expanses of bare wall and maximizing plantings where growing space is limited. Wall containers may be of solid construction – literally, a pot flattened on one side with a fixing point for attachment – or of open ironwork.

CHECKLIST

■ **Container styles** Wall pots are made from a variety of materials, from terra cotta to metal. Remember that unusual, decorative shapes may be awkward to plant up. If there is no provision for drainage, or no room for root development, use the pot as an outer vessel and plant up a more suitable, lightweight container that will fit inside.

■ **Fixing** Make sure that the method of fixing provided is sufficient to support the planted pot safely. Where the only fixing is a single hole in the back of the pot, add small L-shaped or mirror brackets to share the load.

■ **Planting up** When using decorative pots, arrange the plants so that the container itself remains visible – just the opposite of planting up a hanging basket. Remember that the display can only be viewed from one side, and that there is no room for plants to grow or develop at the back of the

CERAMIC ANGLED WALL POT

pot. Open-work mangers should be lined in the same way as hanging baskets (see p. 97).

■ **Watering** Wall containers receive virtually no rain, so make sure that they are within easy reach to allow regular watering.

Plants can be trained through ironwork

WALL MANGER

6

TIPS FOR CHOOSING PLANTS

• Upright plants such as pelargoniums, bush fuchsias, heathers, primulas, and spring-flowering bulbs allow a highly decorated wall pot to remain visible once planted up.

• Avoid using very tall plants that are out of proportion to the depth of the pot.

• One or two strands of ivy or a similar trailing plant will help to soften the outline without obscuring the container; stems can be cut back to the base if they start to become untidy looking.

• Where pots are of specific and unusual designs, it can be fun to try to find a particularly appropriate plant for them. A classical style, stonework face, for example, is a popular design; plant it up with the fine-textured blue grass *Festuca glauca* to give it a shock of steely blue "hair." A lion's mask can be provided with a golden "mane" of creeping jenny (*Lysimachia nummularia* 'Aurea'): pinch the shoots back regularly so that the stems frame the head rather than cover it.

CREEPING JENNY

GOLDEN CREEPING JENNY

6

INDEX

ACKNOWLEDGEMENTS

p. 9 Jerry Harpur/designer Helen Yemem; p. 15 Jerry Harpur/designer Lisette Pleasance, London;
p. 16 Steven Wooster/designer Geoffrey Whiten; p. 19 Jerry Harpur/designer Isabelle Green, California;
p. 21 Steven Wooster/designer Terence Conran; p. 24 Andrew Lawson/designer Anthony Noel;
p. 30 Steven Wooster/designer Carol Klein; p. 31 Steven Wooster/designer Terence Conran; p. 33 Steven
Wooster/designer Carol Klein; p. 34 John Glover; p. 36, p. 37 Steven Wooster/deisgner Terence Conran;
p. 39 Steven Wooster/designer Chris Gregory; p. 57 Jerry Harpur/designer Anne Alexander-Sinclair;
p. 58 Andrew Lawson; p. 63 Jerry Harpur/designer Edwina von Gal, New York City; p. 70 Andrew
Lawson; p. 72 Steven Wooster/Fairweather Sculpture; p. 76 Steven Wooster/designer Carol Klein; p. 92
Marcus Harpur/designer Susan Rowley; p. 93 Marcus Harpur/designer Susan Rowley; p. 107 John Glover;
p. 108 John Glover. Thanks to Tim Stansfield; Country Gardens, Tring; Jane Haley-Pursey and staff
at Solesbridge Mill Water Gardens, Chorleywood; and Spear and Jackson.